Exploring TECHNOLOGY

11

Index

Marshall Cavendish
New York • London • Toronto • Sydney

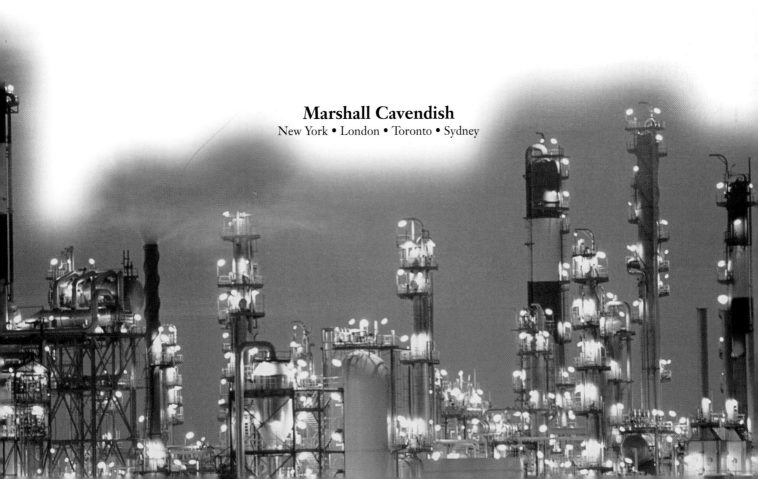

Marshall Cavendish
99 White Plains Road
Tarrytown, New York 10591

www.marshallcavendish.com

© 2004 Marshall Cavendish Corporation

Created by **The Brown Reference Group plc**

Library of Congress Cataloging-in-Publication Data

Exploring technology.
    p. cm.
    Includes bibliographical references and index.
  Contents: v. 1. ABR-BIC -- v. 2. BIO-COG -- v. 3. COL-END -- v. 4.
ENE-GEO -- v. 5. GLA-LEA -- v. 6. LIG-MOV -- v. 7. MUL-POT -- v. 8.
POW-SHI -- v. 9. SHI-TEL -- v. 10. TEL-WOO -- v. 11. Index.
  ISBN 0-7614-7406-4 (set)
  1. Technology--Encyclopedias.
  T9 .E97 2003
  603--dc21

                              2002071510
  ISBN 0-7614-7406-4 (set)
  ISBN 0-7614-7417-X (vol 11)

Printed in China

08 07 06 05 04 03 5 4 3 2 1

PHOTOGRAPHIC CREDITS

CERN Geneva: *814;* **Digital Vision:** *824-825, 830-831;* **Dunlop Tyres Ltd.:** *815;* **DuPont:** *817;*
NASA: *804,* Kennedy Space Center *821;* **Siemens AG:** *819;* **U.S. Library of Congress:** *818;* **U.S.
National Archives:** *816*

Front cover Corbis
Title page Digital Vision
Contents page Digital Vision

MARSHALL CAVENDISH

Project editor: Peter Mavrikis
Production manager: Alan Tsai
Editorial director: Paul Bernabeo

THE BROWN REFERENCE GROUP PLC

Project editor: Clive Carpenter
Deputy editor: Jim Martin
Design: Richard Berry, Alison Gardner
Picture research: Helen Simm, Susannah Jayes, Rebecca Cox
Illustrations: Darren Awuah, Dax Fullbrook, Mark Walker
Index: Kay Ollerenshaw
Managing editor: Bridget Giles

Exploring TECHNOLOGY

11

Index

Marshall Cavendish
New York • London • Toronto • Sydney

Weights and Measures

IMPERIAL TO METRIC

WEIGHT
Multiply:
__ ounces by 28.35 to get __ grams (g)
__ pounds by 0.454 to get __ kilograms (kg)
__ tons by .907 to get __ metric tons

VOLUME
Multiply:
__ quarts by 0.9461 to get __ liters

TEMPERATURE
First subtract 32 from the Fahrenheit (°F) number, then multiply by 0.5556 to get the Celsius (°C; centigrade) number.

LENGTH
Multiply:
__ inches by 25.4 to get __ millimeters (mm)
__ inches by 2.54 to get __ centimeters (cm)
__ feet by 0.305 to get __ meters (m)
__ miles by 1.609 to get __ kilometers (km)

AREA
Multiply:
__ sq feet by 0.093 to get __ sq meters (sq m)
__ acres by 0.405 to get __ hectares (ha)
__ sq miles by 2.59 to get __ sq kilometers

Imagining a million

The planets, stars, and the spaces between them are so huge that it requires a leap of the imagination to understand the distances involved. Sometimes it can help to break down a large distance, such as a million miles, into more familiar chunks. Imagine that a person travels 25 miles on the day she is born—and every day after that. When she is 109 years old, she will have traveled 1,000,000 miles.

Imagining one-millionth

The most powerful electron microscopes can magnify an object one million times. An object magnified in this way is one-millionth the size

Saturn orbits the Sun at an average distance of 9.54 AU. The nearest of its 30 moons orbits the planet at a distance of 83,400 miles (133,600 km).

METRIC TO IMPERIAL

WEIGHT
Multiply:
__ grams (g) by 0.035 to get __ ounces
__ kilograms (kg) by 2.2 to get __ pounds
__ metric tons by 1.102 to get __ tons

VOLUME
Multiply:
__ liters (l) by 1.057 to get __ quarts

TEMPERATURE
First multiply the Celsius (°C; centigrade) number by 1.80, then add 32 to get the Fahrenheit (°F) number.

LENGTH
Multiply:
__ millimeters (mm) by 0.039 to get __ inches
__ centimeters (cm) by 0.39 to get __ inches
__ meters (m) by 3.28 to get __ feet
__ kilometers (km) by 0.621 to get __ miles

AREA
Multiply:
__ sq meters (sq m) by 10.764 to get __ sq feet
__ hectares (ha) by 2.47 to get __ acres

---

of the image. Just one of the miles that person traveled is one-millionth ($\frac{1}{1,000,000}$) of the total distance. Large distances are often expressed in astronomical units (AU) or light-years. An AU is the average distance between Earth and the Sun. One AU = 93,000,000 miles (or 149,600,000 km).

It takes about eight minutes for the light from the Sun to travel to Earth. However, that distance is very small in terms of the Universe. One light-year is the distance a light beam would travel through a vacuum (a space without matter) in one year. One light-year = 5,878,000,000,000 miles = 9,460,500,000,000 km = 63,240 AU.

Weight
1 gram (1 g) = 1 paper clip
   1 kilogram (1 kg) = 1,000 g
      = 8 bananas

Temperature
Water boils at 212°F or 100°C
Water freezes at 32°F or 0°C
Body temperature is 98.6°F or 37°C

Area
1 acre = a football field without the end zones
1 square mile = 640 acres
(Washington, D.C., covers 67 square miles.)

Length
1 millimeter (1 mm) = thickness of a penny
1 centimeter (1 cm) = 10 mm
1 meter (1 m) = 100 cm = 1,000 mm

Decimals and Fractions
Decimals are another way of showing fractions.
One-half = ½ = 0.5; one-third = ⅓ = 0.333;
one-quarter = ¼ = 0.25; and one-tenth = ⅒ = 0.1

The Atomic World

Atoms formed from the remains of the Big Bang. The particles scattered by this explosion cooled and were transformed into the subatomic particles that make up all matter today. These grouped to form nuclei (atom centers) surrounded by swarms of electrons. Some 300,000 years after the explosion, the nuclei and electrons grouped to form atoms.

Discovering the atom

The idea that all matter is made up of tiny building blocks called atoms was first proposed by Greek scientist Democritus in the 4th century B.C.E. His theory, however, was overshadowed by fellow Greek Aristotle's theory that matter is made from five elements: air, earth, water, fire, and ether. Not until the 18th and 19th centuries did scientists prove that Democritus was right.

Inside the atom

While Democritus believed atoms to be the smallest particles in the Universe, 19th-century scientists found that atoms consist of three types of particles. These subatomic particles are protons (positive), neutrons (no charge), and electrons (negative). Protons and neutrons make up nearly all the mass of an atom, clustered in a nucleus at the center. Negatively charged electrons, only ½,₀₀₀ the mass of a proton, orbit the nucleus in clouds at different distances.

Subatomic forces

The forces that hold atoms together depend on tiny particles that are exchanged back and forth between protons, neutrons, and electrons. Splitting the nucleus of an atom, called nuclear fission, releases huge amounts of energy, which has been used in power plants and to make bombs. The behavior of subatomic particles is studied in particle accelerators, which fire beams of particles at one another. The particles split when they collide. There are, however, particles that are thought to be truly indivisible. These include electrons and particles called quarks, which make up protons and neutrons.

States of matter

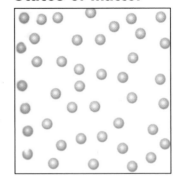

Gas

Atoms can exist singly in some gases, but in most they group together as molecules. Gas molecules are separate and are moving constantly.

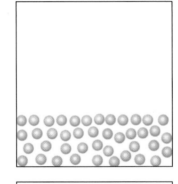

Liquid

In a liquid, the atoms or molecules attract each other and remain close together. They can slide around each other, making the liquid flow.

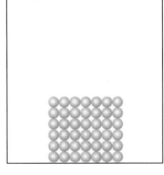

Solid

In most solids, the atoms attract each other strongly and form regular patterns. Force is required to break the bonds and split a solid.

Protons and neutrons

The protons and neutrons in the nucleus of an atom are made up of smaller particles called quarks, which exchange particles called gluons. This exchange exerts a force that prevents the protons and neutrons from flying apart.

Neutrons are particles with no charge

Positively charged protons

Discovering the nucleus

New Zealand physicist Ernest Rutherford discovered the nucleus of the atom by firing tiny alpha particles at a sheet of gold foil. Most of the particles passed through, showing that the atoms in the gold are mostly empty space. However, some of these positively charged particles bounced back as if they had encountered a positively charged mass. These were the nuclei of the gold atoms.

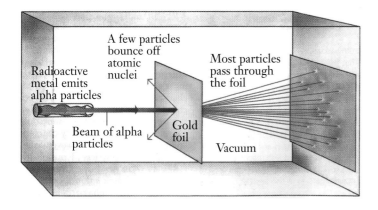

Radioactive metal emits alpha particles

A few particles bounce off atomic nuclei

Most particles pass through the foil

Beam of alpha particles

Gold foil

Vacuum

Nuclear fission

Fission begins when a neutron collides with the nucleus of an atom, for example, uranium 235. This atom nucleus splits into two smaller nuclei and more lone neutrons, releasing huge amounts of energy, called nuclear radiation.

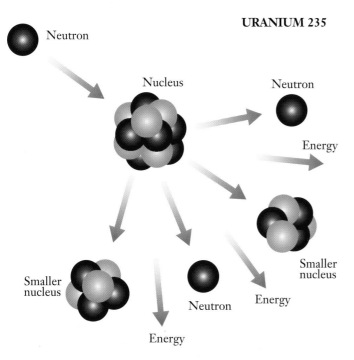

URANIUM 235

Neutron

Nucleus

Neutron

Energy

Smaller nucleus

Smaller nucleus

Neutron

Energy

Energy

Sharing electrons

Some molecules form when atoms share electrons. Three hydrogen atoms bond in this way with one nitrogen atom to form a pyramid-shaped molecule of ammonia—a pungent, colorless gas.

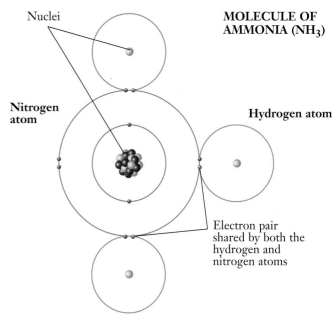

Nuclei

MOLECULE OF AMMONIA (NH_3)

Nitrogen atom

Hydrogen atom

Electron pair shared by both the hydrogen and nitrogen atoms

Polar molecules

Atoms have a positively charged nucleus at their center, surrounded by negatively charged electrons. Some atoms attract electrons more strongly than others. When a molecule contains two types of atoms, electrons from one are often pulled toward the other, making a polar molecule.

Nonpolar hydrogen (H_2) molecule

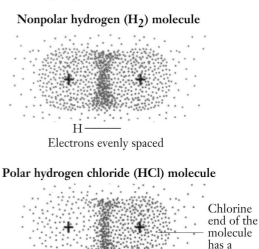

H ———
Electrons evenly spaced

Polar hydrogen chloride (HCl) molecule

Chlorine end of the molecule has a negative charge

H ——— Cl
Electrons unevenly spaced

Periodic Table

The periodic table classifies chemical elements according to their properties and increasing atomic weight. The first element in the table is hydrogen, the lightest element. There are at least 115 known elements, but some have existed only for a short time in the laboratory. The most recently produced elements (110 to 112, 114, 116, and 118) are not yet officially named.

The metals in the **transition series** share similar properties. As with all elements, their chemical properties result from the electron structure of their atoms. However, ions of these metals can hold a varying number of electrons and can therefore make many different compounds, with several vibrant colors.

Metals

An opaque, shiny substance that is a good conductor of electricity and heat.

Metalloid

A substance that is half metal, half nonmetal. Many are semiconductors that can stop and start a current of electricity.

Nonmetal

Element that does not share the properties of metals. Nonmetals readily gain electrons to form negative ions and they are poor conductors of heat and electricity.

Hydrogen is the first element in the first group of the table. More than 90% of atoms in the Universe are hydrogen. Under usual conditions, hydrogen exists as a diatomic molecule (H_2)—a very light, explosive gas.

Transition series

	1	2		3	4	5	6	7	8
1	1 H 1.0079								
2	3 Li 6.941	4 Be 9.0122							
3	11 Na 22.990	12 Mg 24.305		3	4	5	6	7	8
4	19 K 39.098	20 Ca 40.078		21 Sc scandium	22 Ti titanium	23 V vanadium	24 Cr chromium	25 Mn manganese	26 Fe iron
5	37 Rb 85.468	38 Sr 87.62		39 Y yttrium	40 Zr zirconium	41 Nb niobium	42 Mo molybdenum	43 Tc technetium	44 Ru ruthenium
6	55 Cs 132.91	56 Ba 137.33	57-70 *	71 Lu lutetium	72 Hf hafnium	73 Ta tantalum	74 W tungsten	75 Re rhenium	76 Os osmium
7	87 Fr [223.02]	88 Ra [226.03]	89-102 †	103 Lr lawrencium	104 Rf rutherfordium	105 Db dubnium	106 Sg seaborgium	107 Bh bohrium	108 Hs hassium

The **alkali metals** are in Group 1 of the table. They include highly reactive metals such as sodium and potassium. These metals readily react with acids and they are mainly found in nature as ionic salt compounds.

* Lanthanide series	57 La lanthanum	58 Ce cerium	59 Pr praesodymium	60 Nd neodymium	61 Pm promethium	62 Sm samarium
† Actinide series	89 Ac actinium	90 Th thorium	91 Pa protactinium	92 U uranium	93 Np neptunium	94 Pu plutonium

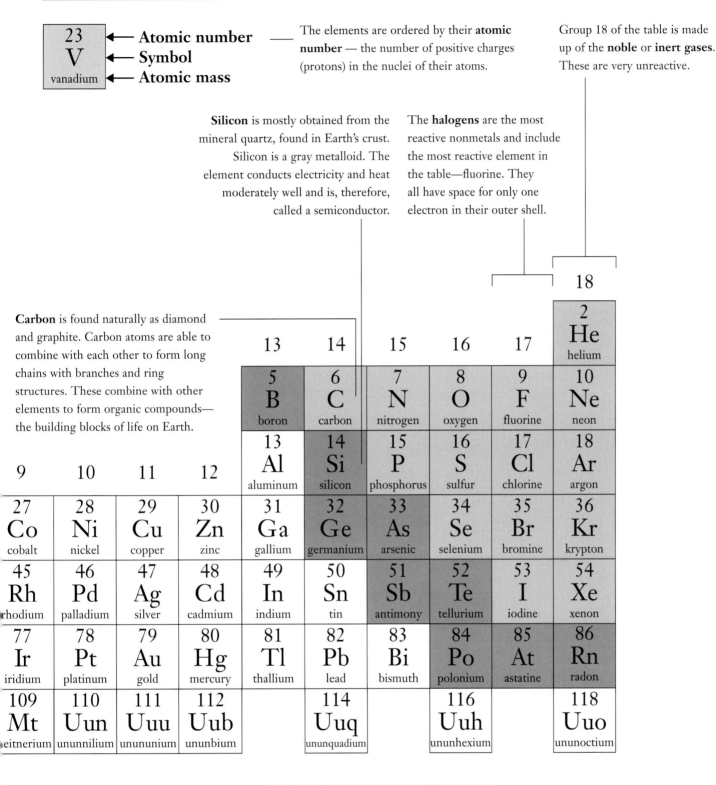

23
V
vanadium

← **Atomic number**
← **Symbol**
← **Atomic mass**

The elements are ordered by their **atomic number** — the number of positive charges (protons) in the nuclei of their atoms.

Group 18 of the table is made up of the **noble** or **inert gases**. These are very unreactive.

Silicon is mostly obtained from the mineral quartz, found in Earth's crust. Silicon is a gray metalloid. The element conducts electricity and heat moderately well and is, therefore, called a semiconductor.

The **halogens** are the most reactive nonmetals and include the most reactive element in the table—fluorine. They all have space for only one electron in their outer shell.

Carbon is found naturally as diamond and graphite. Carbon atoms are able to combine with each other to form long chains with branches and ring structures. These combine with other elements to form organic compounds—the building blocks of life on Earth.

13	14	15	16	17	18
					2 He helium
5 B boron	6 C carbon	7 N nitrogen	8 O oxygen	9 F fluorine	10 Ne neon
13 Al aluminum	14 Si silicon	15 P phosphorus	16 S sulfur	17 Cl chlorine	18 Ar argon

9	10	11	12						
27 Co cobalt	28 Ni nickel	29 Cu copper	30 Zn zinc	31 Ga gallium	32 Ge germanium	33 As arsenic	34 Se selenium	35 Br bromine	36 Kr krypton
45 Rh rhodium	46 Pd palladium	47 Ag silver	48 Cd cadmium	49 In indium	50 Sn tin	51 Sb antimony	52 Te tellurium	53 I iodine	54 Xe xenon
77 Ir iridium	78 Pt platinum	79 Au gold	80 Hg mercury	81 Tl thallium	82 Pb lead	83 Bi bismuth	84 Po polonium	85 At astatine	86 Rn radon
109 Mt meitnerium	110 Uun ununnilium	111 Uuu unununium	112 Uub ununbium		114 Uuq ununquadium		116 Uuh ununhexium		118 Uuo ununoctium

63 Eu europium	64 Gd gadolinium	65 Tb terbium	66 Dy dysprosium	67 Ho holmium	68 Er erbium	69 Tm thulium	70 Yb ytterbium
95 Am americium	96 Cm curium	97 Bk berkelium	98 Cf californium	99 Es einsteinium	100 Fm fermium	101 Md mendelevium	102 No nobelium

The **actinide elements** are all radioactive metals. Uranium was discovered first, in 1789, and was named for the recently spotted planet, Uranus.

Science Time Line

C. 3000 B.C.E. People study the Sun and other stars. Stonehenge in England is built to mark where the Sun rises and sets at different points in the year.

600 B.C.E. Greek philosopher Thales of Miletus creates a charge that can pick up a feather by rubbing amber with fur. This is static electricity.

5th century B.C.E. In Mesopotamia, early stargazers make star maps and try to predict the future from the movement of the stars.

460–370 B.C.E. Greek scientist Democritus suggests that all matter is made up of particles called atoms.

1705 Using Newton's ideas about gravity, English astronomer Edmond Halley realizes that the comets seen in 1531, 1607, and 1682 are the same comet. Halley's comet is seen again, as he predicts, in 1758.

1687 English scientist Isaac Newton publishes the *Principia*. It describes how gravity keeps the planets in orbit around the Sun.

1620 English philosopher Francis Bacon points out that South America and Africa would fit together. This suggests the two were once joined.

1610 Invention of the telescope. Galileo builds his own and spots Jupiter's moons. The moons show that not every object in space revolves around Earth.

1781 German-born astronomers William Herschel and his sister Caroline discover the planet Uranus using a giant, home-made telescope.

1803 English scientist John Dalton identifies 33 elements. He also explains how chemical reactions take place through the exchange of atoms.

1840s English scientist James Joule shows how energy can be converted from one form into another. He builds a paddle wheel that heats the water slightly.

1831–1875 Scottish scientist James Clerk Maxwell suggests that visible light is one of many types of electromagnetic radiation, all traveling at the speed of light.

1930 Pluto, the most distant planet in Earth's Solar System, is discovered.

1927 Belgian astronomer Georges Lemaître proposes that the Universe was once packed into a tiny point that exploded in the Big Bang and is still expanding.

1923 U.S. astronomer Edwin Hubble discovers far-off galaxies. He notices that their stars appear red. This "redshift" shows galaxies are moving away from us.

1919 Einstein's theory that light is affected by gravity is proved during a solar eclipse. Scientists observe the deflection of a distant star's light near the Sun.

1934 U.S. naturalist Charles William Beebe develops a spherical diving vessel called the bathysphere and plunges to a record depth of 3,028 feet (923 m). This invention leads to greater knowledge of the ocean depths.

1939–1945 During World War II, U.S. physicists build nuclear bombs. When dropped on Japanese cities Hiroshima and Nagasaki in 1945, they kill 240,000 people.

1960 *TIROS* (Television and Infrared Observation Satellite), the first U.S. weather satellite, is launched.

1961 The USSR launches the first human, Yuri Gagarin, into space, winning the first leg of the space race. U.S. astronauts land on the Moon in 1969.

384–322 B.C.E. Greek philosopher Aristotle teaches that the Universe is made up of mixtures of elements: air, earth, fire, water, and ether.

200 B.C.E. Greek astronomer Eratosthenes decides the Earth is shaped like a ball with a circumference of 25,000 miles (40,233 km). This figure was only 200 km off.

150 C.E. Alexandrian astronomer Ptolemy makes a model of the Universe in which the Moon, Sun, and planets revolve around Earth.

1492 Believing the Earth is a ball, Italian explorer Christopher Columbus sets sail west from Spain, aiming to reach Asia. Instead, he reaches the Americas, which lie in the way.

1589 Italian scientist Galileo Galilei shows that all objects are pulled to Earth at the same rate. He drops a heavy and a light object from the top of the Leaning Tower of Pisa.

1582 Pope Gregory XIII has a new calendar drawn up. The Gregorian calendar varies from the true solar year by only 26 seconds.

1543 Polish monk Nicolaus Copernicus introduces the idea that the planets revolve around the Sun, not around the Earth.

1519–1522 Portuguese explorer Ferdinand Magellan circumnavigates (sails around) the globe, proving that the Earth is spherical.

1830s Swiss geologist Louis Agassiz studies rock features in northern Europe and North America. He finds that vast areas were once covered by ice.

1896 French physicist Antoine Henri Becquerel discovers that uranium gives out strong radiation. Polish scientist Marie Curie further investigates this radioactivity.

1897 English physicist J. J. Thomson discovers the electron. He believes an atom is built like a plum pudding, with negative electrons dotted through a positive mass.

1905 German-born U.S. scientist Albert Einstein explains how a very small amount of matter can be converted into a huge amount of energy. This led to the generation of energy by nuclear fission and fusion. $E = mc^2$

1915 German-born U.S. physicist Albert Einstein writes the general theory of relativity. He suggests gravity is caused by a large mass distorting space and time.

1913 Danish chemist Niels Bohr devises a model of the atom with electrons orbiting the nucleus in different energy levels.

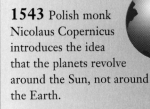

1912 U.S. scientist Victor Hess flies in a hot-air balloon to measure radiation reaching Earth from space. He finds that Earth is bombarded by cosmic rays.

1911 New Zealand-born physicist Ernest Rutherford discovers the nucleus of the atom when he fires particles at a sheet of gold. A few particles bounce back when they hit the gold atoms' nuclei.

1973 U.S. chemists begin to study the effects of chlorofluorocarbons (CFCs) on the atmosphere. In the 1980s, satellite images reveal a hole in the ozone layer.

1986 A reactor explodes at a nuclear power plant in Chernobyl, Ukraine. This causes protests about the use of nuclear power.

1990 Hubble Space Telescope is launched. It looks into the depths of space and makes hundreds of discoveries, including black holes.

2001 and beyond The *International Space Station*, crewed by scientists and astronauts, acts as an orbiting laboratory and docking station for further space exploration.

Inventions Time Line

 C. 500,000 B.C.E. The discovery of fire changes people's lives. Fire provides heat, light, and protection. The invention of cooking follows.

C. 8000 B.C.E. Farming begins. Instead of gathering grain from wild wheat plants, some people in the Middle East plant grain themselves.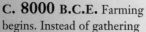

C. 6000 B.C.E. The discovery of how to smelt metals is one of the greatest advances in technology. Metal tools replace stone.

BY 5000 B.C.E. Because Mesopotamia lacks a good building stone supply, its inhabitants invent mud bricks.

 1663 A device that creates an electric spark is made by German scientist Otto von Guericke. His invention is the forerunner of generators.

BY 1600 Zacharias Janssen, a Dutch eyeglass maker, makes the first microscope.

C. 1450 The invention of movable type, by Johannes Gutenberg in Germany, leads to a more rapid spread of knowledge.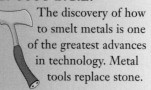

C. 725 C.E The mechanical clock is invented in China. In Europe, clocks are invented independently in the 13th century.

1702–1712 The first practical steam engine, constructed by English engineer Thomas Newcomen, pumps water from mines.

 1709 Iron is smelted successfully with coke. This helps bring a rapid change in industry—the Industrial Revolution.

1800 The voltaic pile, the first battery, is invented in Italy by Alessandro Volta.

 **1805** A refrigerator is devised by U.S. engineer Oliver Evans. The first practical model is made in Germany, in the 1870s.

1939 The first electronic computer is built. Early computers are large, occupying whole rooms.

1926 Scottish scientist John Logie Baird demonstrates television.

1903 The first effective airplane is constructed and flown by Orville and Wilbur Wright.

1895 The first practical system of wireless telegraphy is constructed by Guglielmo Marconi in Italy.

1941 The test flight of the first airplane powered by a jet engine takes place.

1942 The world's first atomic reactor is assembled at the University of Chicago by a team led by Italian-born Enrico Fermi.

1944 German V2 rockets, designed by Werhner von Braun, are launched during World War II (1939–1945).

1947 Three U.S. physicists invent the transistor. These are electronic pathways used to process information in computers.

C. 4000 B.C.E. The wheel is invented. Early wheels are wooden disks. Spoked wheels are invented by c. 2000 B.C.E.

BY 3600 B.C.E. Writing develops, probably in Mesopotamia.

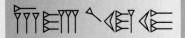

BY 3000 B.C.E. Plows pulled by oxen appear in Egypt and Mesopotamia.

C. 2500 B.C.E. There is evidence of smelting iron to make tools in ancient Egypt. Iron tools are much harder and more durable than earlier bronze ones.

1ST CENTURY C.E. Paper is invented in China by Cai Lun.

400-500 B.C.E. The invention of the stirrup, probably in Central Asia, makes long-distance travel by horse much easier.

C. 1000 B.C.E. The first coins are made in Lydia (modern-day Turkey). Trade increases.

C. 2400 B.C.E. A standardized system of weights and measures, the 60-minute hour and 24-hour day, are introduced in Mesopotamia.

1825 The first public railroad opens in northern England.

1835 U.S. inventor Samuel Morse invents the first working telegraph system.

1861 U.S. inventor Elisha Otis patents a safety device for elevators. This invention makes high-rise buildings possible.

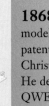

1868 The first workable model of the typewriter is patented by U.S. inventor Christopher Latham Scholes. He devises the standard QWERTY keyboard.

1885–1888 The alternating current (AC) electric motor is developed by Nikola Tesla.

1885 At Mannheim, Germany, the first automobile is unveiled—a three-wheeler constructed by Karl Benz.

1879 The electric lightbulb is invented by U.S. scientist Thomas Alva Edison.

1876 Scottish-born scientist Alexander Graham Bell invents the telephone.

1959 Working independently, two U.S. engineers produce the integrated circuit (the chip). This enables complex electronic machines to be constructed.

1975 The first personal computer is produced.

1980 English scientist Tim Berners-Lee writes a computer program that, in 1991, becomes the common language of the World Wide Web.

2001 The map of the human genome is published. This identifies all the approximately 30,000 genes in human DNA. The 1985 invention of PCR made this possible.

Famous Inventors

Ackerman, Rudolf (1764–1834)
German bookseller who figured out the principle of angled steering arms to ensure the correct turning angle for the wheels of vehicles.

Appert, Nicholas (c. 1750–1841)
French confectioner who invented a method of preserving food in bottles. This process was the forerunner of food canning.

Archimedes (c. 287–212 B.C.E.) Greek scientist and mathematician who invented the conveyor.

Aspdin, Joseph (1799–1855)
English bricklayer who developed the first modern cement, portland cement, in 1824.

Atanasoff, John (1903–1995)
U.S. teacher who built the first electronic computer—the Atanasoff Berry Computer (ABC)—in 1939.

Babbage, Charles (1792–1871)
English mathematician who designed the analytical engine, the first advanced calculator.

Baird, John Logie (1888–1946)
Scottish inventor who, in 1926, was the first to develop and to demonstrate television.

Bardeen, John (1908–1991)
U.S. physicist who won two Nobel Prizes for physics: in 1972 (with Walter Brattain and William Shockley) for research leading to the invention of the transistor and in 1972 for the theory of superconductivity.

Baudot, Emile (1845–1903) French inventor who devised a method of sending more than one telegraph message at once.

Beau de Rochas, Alphonse (1815–1893) French railroad engineer who, in 1862, described the principles of a four-stroke engine but never attempted to build it.

Bell, Alexander Graham (1847–1922) Scottish-born U.S. inventor who constructed instruments to transmit sound in 1875. The following year, he invented the telephone and, in 1877, founded the world's first telephone company.

Benz, Karl (1844–1929) German automobile pioneer who unveiled the first automobile, a three-wheeler, in Mannheim, Germany, in 1885. The vehicle was powered by a water-cooled gas engine. Benz merged his business with that of Gottlieb Daimler, and the corporation later became known as Mercedes-Benz.

Berners-Lee, Tim (born 1955)
English computer scientist who developed the global hypertext computer program that became the World Wide Web.

Bessemer, Henry (1813–1898)
English engineer and inventor who devised a process to mass-produce steel inexpensively. His method introduced air to expel carbon from molten steel. Bessemer had earlier become rich through inventing cheap gilding.

Tim Berners-Lee

Brattain, Walter (1902–1987)
U.S. physicist who, with John Bardeen, coinvented the transistor.

Brunel, Marc Isambard (1769–1849)
French-born British engineer who developed the tunnel shield used to bore tunnels. His son was Isambard Kingdom Brunel (1806–1859), the English railroad, bridge, and marine engineer.

Bushnell, David (c. 1742–1824) U.S. inventor who, in 1776, built the *American Turtle*, the first successful submarine. The craft was used against the British flagship *HMS Eagle* in New York Harbor later in the same year.

Cai Lun (c. 50–c. 118 C.E.) Chinese inventor who was the first person to make paper.

Carlson, Chester (1906–1986)
U.S. physicist who invented xerography (photocopying) in 1938. When his employer rejected his idea, Carlson created his own company to make copiers.

Carothers, Wallace (1896–1936) U.S. chemist who, in 1933–1935, invented nylon. Carothers, who received almost no financial benefit from his invention, suffered from depression and committed suicide.

Cockerell, Christopher (1900–1999)
English engineer who, in retirement, invented the hovercraft.

Cooke, William (1806–1879)
English physicist who developed the telegraph with Charles Wheatstone.

Cousteau, Jacques (1910–1997)
French oceanographer and naval engineer who invented the aqualung in the 1940s. Cousteau increased public interest in underwater life and exploration through his television programs.

Cugnot, Nicholas-Joseph (1725–1804) French artillery officer whose steam-driven carriage, built in 1769, is the earliest recorded steam-powered road vehicle.

Curtiss, Glen (1878–1930) U.S. airplane designer who invented the seaplane.

Daimler, Gottlieb (1834–1900) German engineer who was the principal pioneer of the internal-combustion engine. Daimler did not invent the internal-combustion engine but improved it to make it practical. In 1885, Daimler and his colleague Wilhelm Maybach (1846–1929) patented a four-stroke engine. They made the first motorcycle by installing the engine on a bicycle.

Darby, Abraham (1678–1717) English ironmaster who, in 1709, was the first person to smelt iron ore successfully with coke rather than coal. Darby's invention, coke smelting, was a major factor in the development of the 18th-century Industrial Revolution.

Deere, John (1804–1886) U.S. blacksmith who developed the first successful steel plow in 1837.

De Forest, Lee (1873–1961) U.S. inventor who held more than 180 patents for inventions. In 1906–1907, he invented the triode vacuum tube (which is used in television receivers). He also invented the first successful film projector and the film soundtrack.

Dickson, William (1860–1935) Scottish engineer who coinvented the movie camera. He was a young laboratory assistant working for U.S. inventor Thomas Alva Edison, who commissioned him to develop a device to show moving images.

Diesel, Rudolf (1858–1913) German engineer who built an engine with combustion within a cylinder. He was severely injured when the prototype exploded. In 1897, Diesel produced the first successful working version of his machine, which came to be called a diesel engine.

Dolby, Ray (born 1933) U.S. engineer who developed an electronic device to eliminate noise on recorded sound. Dolby sound is named for him.

Dudley, Dud (1599–1684) English ironmaster who, in 1624, invented the first blast furnace to be heated by coal rather than charcoal.

Dummer, Geoffrey (born 1909) English scientist who was the first to describe the principles of the microchip.

Dunlop, John Boyd (1840–1921) Scottish veterinarian who invented the first practical pneumatic (air-filled) tire in 1888. He developed his tires for his son's bicycle. Dunlop was not the first to invent an air-filled tire: another Scot, Robert William Thomson (1822–1873), patented the idea in the 1840s, but his tires were not successful.

Eastman, George (1854–1932) U.S. entrepreneur and inventor who developed flexible celluloid film (1885). His Eastman Kodak Company introduced the first commercial snapshot camera, the Brownie, in 1900.

Eckert, J. Presper (1919–1995) U.S. engineer who, with John Mauchly, invented ENIAC, the first large general-purpose electronic computer, in the mid-1940s.

Edison, Thomas Alva (1847–1931) U.S. inventor who registered 1,093 inventions. Edison invented the phonograph (1877), the electric light bulb (1870-1879), and developed the first power plant. He invented the

John Dunlop

the kinetoscope, a successful motion picture camera, and synchronized this and his phonograph to produce moving talking pictures. Edison was taught at home because of a severe hearing problem and set up a laboratory in the basement when he was aged 10. He opened the first private research station and laboratory in the United States at Menlo Park, New Jersey, in 1876.

Evinrude, Ole (1877–1934) Norwegian-born U.S. engineer who designed the first outboard motor.

Faraday, Michael (1791–1867) English scientist whose induction ring (1831) was the ancestor of the transformer, the device that controls variations of voltage and current.

Fermi, Enrico (1901–1954) Italian-born U.S. physicist who invented the nuclear reactor in 1942. He received the Nobel Prize for discovering new radioactive elements.

Fleming, J. Ambrose (1849–1945) English physicist who invented the two-electrode valve, which became known as the diode. This valve was important in the development of radio.

Ford, Henry (1863–1947) U.S. industrialist who, in 1908, invented industrial mass production when production of the black Model T Ford automobile began.

Foudrinier, Henry (1766–1854) and **Sealy** (1774–1847) English brothers and manufacturers who developed the papermaking machine that is named for them.

Francis, James (1815–1892) U.S.-born British hydraulic engineer who invented the mixed-flow Francis turbine, which is used to produce hydroelectricity.

Franklin, Benjamin (1706–1790) U.S. statesman, philosopher, and inventor who invented the lightning rod to protect buildings from damage by lightning.

Fulton, Robert (1765–1815) U.S. engineer who developed the first successful steamboat, the *Clermont*, in 1807. Fulton did not invent the steamboat but was the first to put the idea into practice.

Gabor, Dennis (1900–1979) Hungarian-born British physicist who invented holography in the late 1940s. The technology to make holography a practical possibility was still more than 20 years away.

Galilei, Galileo (1564–1642) Italian astronomer, mathematician, and philosopher who made the first thermometer. He is sometimes,

Thomas Alva Edison

wrongly, credited with the invention of the telescope. In 1632, he was convicted of heresy for supporting the idea of a Sun-centered solar system and was held under house arrest for the rest of his life.

Gesner, Abraham (1797–1864) Canadian geologist who figured out a way to distill kerosene.

Gibbon, John H. (1903–1973) U.S. doctor who invented the heart-lung machine to support the heart and lungs during surgery.

Goddard, Robert (1882–1945) U.S. engineer who pioneered longer-range rockets and held more than 200 patents for rocketry inventions. In 1935, Goddard was the first to launch a liquid-propellant rocket. Goddard's achievements were not acknowledged until after his death, but he is now recognized as the father of modern rocketry.

Goodyear, Charles (1800–1860) U.S. inventor who discovered the vulcanization process to harden rubber when he accidentally dropped a rubber-sulfur mixture on a hot stove. Goodyear patented vulcanization in 1844.

Gutenberg, Johannes (c. 1400–1468) German inventor whose development of movable type, in around 1450, helped speed the spread of ideas through printing. Gutenberg used hand-set type cast in molds. Movable type had previously been developed independently in eastern Asia but not widely used.

Harrison, John (1693–1776) English carpenter who invented the chronometer, a clock that could keep accurate time at sea. This enabled mariners to calculate longitude.

Henry, Beulah (1888–1973) U.S. inventor whose 49 patents included a vacuum ice cream freezer.

Hertz, Heinrich (1857–1894) German physicist who invented the resonator to generate and transmit electromagnetic radiation. The hertz, the unit of measurement for radio and electrical frequencies, is named for him.

Holabird, William (1854–1923) U.S. architect who, in partnership with Martin Roche (1855–1927), invented the steel-frame type of skyscraper.

Howe, Elias (1819–1867) U.S. textile worker who made the first practical sewing machine in 1845. After receiving little interest in his invention in the United States, Howe went to England. Upon his return, Howe found that his ideas had been copied and had to begin lawsuits to get his patent upheld.

Hussey, Obed (1792–1860) U.S. inventor who was a pioneer of the reaping machine.

Huygens, Christiaan (1629–1695) Dutch physicist, astronomer, and mathematician who made the first pendulum clock. Huygens discovered the first moon of Saturn and the nature of the rings of Saturn.

Jacquard, Joseph-Marie (1752–1834) French inventor who designed an automatic loom that used punch cards to control patterns. Jacquard's punch cards were later used in mechanical calculators.

Janssen, Zacharias (1580–1638) Dutch optical instrument maker and engineer who, when probably less than 20 years of age, made the first microscope while working for his father's business.

Jenner, Edward (1749–1823) English country doctor who, in 1796, invented vaccination. Observing that dairymaids did not catch smallpox, he inoculated patients with cowpox virus. This built up immunity against the deadly disease smallpox.

Jones, Amanda (1835–1914) U.S. inventor who devised the vacuum method of canning. She also invented a safety valve for oil pipes.

Kettering, Charles (1876–1958) U.S. engineer who invented the self-starter for automobile engines, an engine-driver generator, and the electric cash register.

Kilby, Jack (born 1923) U.S. electrical engineer who invented the first practical electronic chip. U.S. engineer Robert Noyce also invented the chip independently.

Kurzweil, Raymond (born 1952) U.S. scientist and engineer who invented the first print-to-speech reading machine for the blind.

Kwolek, Stephanie (born 1923) U.S. chemist who invented Kevlar, a material used for bulletproof vests.

Lamarr, Hedy (Hedwig Kiesler; 1913–2000) Austrian-born U.S. actress who, with U.S. musician George Antheil (1900–1959), invented spread-spectrum (or frequency hopping), originally a method to control armed torpedoes over long distances. The technology has since been adapted to allow microprocessors to communicate at distance.

Laval, Carl de (1845–1913) Swedish engineer who developed the first centrifuge in 1878. His machine separated cream from milk.

Leclanché, Georges (1839–1882) French engineer who, in 1866, used zinc and carbon electrodes to make the first dry-cell battery. His invention is still widely used.

Leonardo da Vinci (1452–1519) Italian artist, scientist, and inventor whose drawings and writings include prototypes of helicopters, armored tanks, and parachutes. Leonardo also invented the minute hand on the clock. Best known as a painter, his works include the *Mona Lisa*. He never published his ideas, but his notebooks later proved an inspiration to scientists and inventors. Leonardo was also an architect and a mathematician and made observations in astronomy, zoology, anatomy, and geology.

Lippershey, Hans (c. 1570–c. 1619) Dutch eyeglass maker who, in 1608, was the first person to apply for a patent for a telescope. Two other Dutchmen have been identified as the possible inventor of the telescope, but Lippershey is usually given credit.

Lovelace, Ada, Countess of (1815–1852) English mathematician who, in the 1840s, devised a program for Charles Babbage's calculating machine. ADA, the software language, is named for her. She was the daughter of English poet Lord Byron (1788–1824).

Lumière, Auguste (1862–1954) and **Louis** (1864–1948) French brothers and film pioneers who, in 1895, devised the cinematographe, the first successful projector.

McCormick, Cyrus (1809–1884) U.S. inventor who, continuing work begun by his father, developed the first reaping machine in 1831.

Macintosh, Charles (1766–1843) Scottish inventor who developed rubberized waterproof material in 1823. The macintosh coat is named for him.

Marconi, Guglielmo (1874–1937) Italian engineer who, in 1895, devised the first practical system of wireless telegraphy. Finding little interest in his invention in Italy, Marconi moved to England, where he was granted the first wireless telegraphy patent in 1896. In 1898, he transmitted a radio message across the English Channel, and in 1901, he transmitted a message across the Atlantic from Cornwall, England, to Newfoundland.

Marrison, Warren (1896–1980) Canadian engineer who, in 1938, invented the quartz-crystal timekeeping mechanism.

Marsh, Sylvester (1803–1884) U.S. industrialist and engineer who was one of the founders of the Chicago meatpacking industry. Marsh invented the cog railroad.

Martin, Pierre-Emile (1824–1915) French steelmaker who, in 1864, invented a method to mix scrap and pig-iron in an open hearth furnace to produce steel.

Mauchly, John (1907–1980) U.S. engineer who, with J. Presper Eckert, coinvented ENIAC, the first large general-purpose electronic computer, in the 1940s.

Midgely, Thomas (1889–1944) U.S. chemist who invented a non-poisonous non-flammable refrigerant—the first of the CFCs, which were later discovered to damage Earth's ozone layer.

Moog, Robert (born 1934) U.S. inventor who invented the electronic music synthesizer in 1963–1964.

Morse, Samuel (1791–1872) U.S. portrait artist and inventor who, in 1835, devised the first working telegraph system. Morse did not have the resources to build his telegraph system and was helped by

Stephanie Kwolek

Samuel Morse

friends, one of whom—U.S. inventor Alfred Vail (1780–1864)—may have invented the key used to transmit the signal. In 1837, Morse patented the telegraph and the code that was later named for him. In 1843, he constructed the first telegraph line in the United States—from Baltimore to Washington, D.C.

Neilson, James B. (1792–1865) Scottish inventor who, in 1828, devised the process of heating the air before it was blown into a blast furnace. This greatly reduced the amount of fuel used in the furnace.

Newcomen, Thomas (1663–1729) English engineer who invented the first practical steam engine in 1705–1712. Newcomen's engine, which was designed to pump water from mines, was the first to use a piston in a cylinder.

Nipkow, Paul (1860–1940) German engineer who, while still a student in 1884, invented a device to scan images for transmission. The device, the Nipkow disk, dissected an image and transmitted it in phases. This was the first step toward the development of television.

Nobel, Alfred (1833–1896) Swedish industrialist who invented the explosive dynamite in 1866. He left money in his will to fund annual science, literary, and peace prizes that bear his name.

Noyce, Robert (1927–1990) U.S. electrical engineer who invented the first practical electronic chip independently from Jack Kilby.

O'Brien, Willis (1886–1962) U.S. movie animator who devised stop-motion animation, where a miniature model is repositioned and rephotographed repeatedly to give the illusion of movement.

Otis, Elisha Graves (1811–1861) U.S. engineer who devised a brake system that made elevators safe. This invention made high-rise buildings possible and changed the skylines of cities worldwide.

Otto, Nikolaus (1832–1891) German engineer who was a pioneer of the internal combustion engine. By 1876, Otto produced a four-stroke engine, but his patent for the engine was canceled when it was discovered that French inventor Alphonse Beau de Rochas had already described, but not built, a similar engine.

Palladio, Andrea (1508–1580) Italian architect who invented the truss bridge, supported by straight beams.

Papin, Denis (1647–1712) French inventor who assisted Christiaan Huygens. Papin developed a machine in which a piston moved by steam action.

Parsons, Charles (1854–1931) English engineer who held more than 300 patents. He invented the steam turbine and turbo-generator. Parsons built the first full-sized ship powered by a steam turbine, the *Turbinia*. This vessel became the fastest ship afloat.

Pascal, Blaise (1623–1662) French mathematician and philosopher who, in 1642, devised a mechanical calculator using a series of wheels. Pascal later conducted experiments on atmospheric pressure.

Pelton, Lester (1829–1918) U.S. engineer who devised the water turbine, the Pelton wheel, which is used in hydroelectric plants.

Pixii, Antoine-Hippolyte (1808–1835) French instrument maker who, in 1832, built the first practical electrical dynamo.

Poulsen, Valdemar (1869–1942) Danish engineer who invented a radio transmitter that produced clear signals. He also produced a system to record and play back telephone messages, the ancestor of voicemail.

Riva-Ricci, Scipione (1863–1937) Italian physician who invented the sphygmomanometer, an instrument for measuring blood pressure.

Robert, Nicholas-Louis (1761–1828) French inventor who developed the first papermaking machine.

Savery, Thomas (c. 1650–1716) English engineer who, in 1698, patented the first steam engine, which pumped water from mines.

Schickard, Wilhelm (1592–1635) German cleric, astronomer, and mathematician who, in 1632, invented a calculating machine.

Scholes, Christopher Latham (1819–1890) U.S. inventor who devised the QWERTY keyboard. In 1868, he patented the first workable model of the typewriter.

Senefelder, Aloys (1819–1890) German playwright who invented the printing process lithography. He became involved in printing after his printers dishonored an agreement to publish one of his plays.

Shockley, William (1910–1989) U.S. physicist who laid the foundations for the invention of the transistor. His research extended knowledge of semiconductors. Unfortunately, Shockley is also known for his extreme views.

Siemens, William (1823–1893) and **Friedrich** (1826–1904) German-born British brothers, who, in 1856, developed the open hearth furnace, which is used in the steel and glassmaking industries.

Sikorsky, Igor (1889–1972) Ukrainian-born U.S. scientist and engineer who invented the first practical helicopter in 1939.

Spangler, James Murray (1848–1915) U.S. janitor who produced an elementary vacuum cleaner to help him overcome his allergy to dust. In 1907, he sold the patent for his invention to U.S. industrialist William Hoover (1849–1932), and vacuums have been widely known as "hoovers" ever since.

Sperry, Elmer (1860–1930) U.S. engineer who held more than 350 patents for inventions. Sperry invented the gyroscopic compass, which was the forerunner of naval autopilot steering systems and of rocket control systems.

Stirling, Robert (1790–1878) Scottish cleric and engineer who invented the external combustion engine, the Stirling engine.

Strowger, Almon (1839–1902) U.S. undertaker who invented the automatic telephone dial system. Almon devised his system in 1891 when he discovered that local telephone operators were routing business calls to competitors.

Sturgeon, William (1783–1850) English inventor who devised the first electromagnet in 1825.

Svedberg, Theodor (1884–1971) Swedish chemist who developed the ultracentrifuge in 1924. To eliminate friction between the rotor and the surrounding air, he pumped the air out of the casing of his centrifuge.

Tesla, Nikola (1856–1943) Serb-U.S. inventor who registered about 700 inventions for which he received little financial benefit. Tesla invented the alternating current (AC) motor and the Tesla coil to generate and receive radio waves. His work also laid the foundations for radar and fluorescent lighting.

Thimmonier, Barthélémy (1793–1857) French tailor who, in 1830, invented the first sewing machine. His machines were destroyed by a mob of tailors who saw the machine as a threat to their employment.

van Drebbel, Cornelius (1572–1633) Dutch inventor who, in 1620–1624, devised a wooden boat that could be rowed underwater.

Volta, Count Alessandro (1745–1827) Italian physicist who invented the voltaic pile, the first electrical battery, in 1800. Volta's battery used disks of copper and silver for electrodes, separated by pasteboard.

von Braun, Wernher (1912–1977) German-born U.S. space scientist who led the German team that developed the V2 rocket used in World War II (1939–1945). After the war, von Braun worked in the United States developing military rockets. He transferred to the space agency NASA and was the architect of the Saturn V launch vehicle.

von Guericke, Otto (1602–1686) German engineer who, in 1663, built the first device able to create an electric spark.

Watson-Watt, Robert (1892–1973) Scottish physicist who devised the first radar set (1915–1916). His invention was not used until he built radar stations to detect airplanes in World War II (1939–1945).

Watt, James (1736–1819) Scottish engineer who invented a more efficient steam engine that used less steam after he had repaired Thomas Newcomen's engine.

Westinghouse, George (1846–1914) U.S. inventor who held 361 patents for inventions, including the air brake, a high-speed vertical steam engine, and an automatic electric signal for the railroad.

Wheatstone, Charles (1802–1875) English physicist who developed the electric telegraph in 1837.

Whitehead, Robert (1828–1905) English engineer who invented the torpedo.

Whitney, Eli (1765–1825) U.S. inventor who developed the cotton gin, which transformed the U.S. textile industry. Because the design was pirated, Whitney made little money from his invention.

Whittle, Frank (1906–1996) English air force officer who coinvented the jet engine. The test flight of the first airplane powered by a jet engine took place in 1941.

Wright, Orville (1871–1948) U.S. aviator who, with his brother, **Wilbur** (1867–1912), constructed the first effective airplane. In 1903, the Wright brothers made the first powered flight.

Yale, Linus, Jr. (1821–1868) U.S. locksmith who devised the lock that bears his name.

Zeppelin, Count Ferdinand von (1838–1917) German general who developed the world's first rigid airship in 1900.

Zworykin, Vladimir (1889–1982) Russian-born U.S. engineer who, in 1929, demonstrated an electronic scanning system to transmit television sound and pictures.

William Siemens

Places to Go

PLACES TO GO BY STATE

Alabama
U.S. Space and Rocket Center
Huntsville
☎ (800) 637-7223
http://www.ussrc.com

Arizona
Arizona Science Center
Phoenix
☎ (602) 716-2000
http://www.azscience.org

California
Computer History Museum
Mountain View
☎ (650) 604-2579
http://www.computerhistory.org

The Exploratorium
San Francisco
☎ (415) 561-0360
http://www.exploratorium.edu

Lawrence Hall of Science
Berkeley
☎ (510) 642-7723
http://www.lhs.berkeley.edu

The Tech Museum of Innovation
San Jose
☎ (510) 594-1400
http://www.thetech.org

Colorado
*The Wings Over the Rockies
Air and Space Museum*
Denver
☎ (303) 360-5360

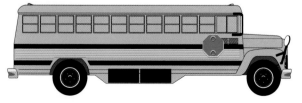

District of Columbia
*National Air and Space
Museum, Smithsonian
Institute*
☎ (202) 357-2700
http://www.si.edu

Florida
Kennedy Space Center
Cape Canaveral
☎ (321) 452-2121
http://www.kennedyspacecenter.com

Illinois
Museum of Science and Industry
Chicago
☎ (773) 684-1414
http://www.msichicago.org

Indiana
Indiana Medical History Museum
Indianapolis
☎ (317) 232-1637

Maryland
Maryland Science Center
Baltimore
☎ (410) 685-5225
http://www.mdsci.org

Massachusetts
*Women of Science
Marine Biology Laboratory*
Woods Hole
☎ (508) 548-3705
http://www.mbl.edu

Museum of Science
Boston
☎ (617) 589-0245
http://www.mos.org

Michigan
Impression 5 Science Center
Lansing
☎ (517) 485-8116

New Jersey
Liberty Science Center
Jersey City
☎ (201) 200-1000
http://www.lsc.org

New Mexico
International Space Hall of Fame
Alamogordo
☎ (505) 437-2840

National Atomic Museum
Albuquerque
☎ (505) 845-6670
http://www.atomicmuseum.com

Ohio
National Inventors Hall of Fame
Akron
☎ (330) 762-4463
http://www.invent.org

Pennsylvania
Carnegie Science Center
Pittsburgh
☎ (412) 237-3400
http://www.carnegiesciencecenter.org

Texas
The Science Place
Tyler
☎ (214) 428-5555
http://www.scienceplace.org

Washington
Pacific Science Center
Seattle
☎ (206) 443-2001
http://www.pscsci.org

Canada
Aero Space Museum of Calgary
☎ (403) 250-3752
http://www.asmac.ab.ca

The Ontario Science Center
Toronto
☎ (888) 696-1010
http://www.osc.on.ca

United Kingdom
National Railway Museum
York
http://nrm.org.uk

Science Museum
London
http://www.nmsi.ac.uk

Visitors to Kennedy Space Center view models, displays, and animations of space missions. Visitors also tour Cape Canaveral and view rockets.

Things to Do

BOOKS

**Earth and Space
(Starting Point Science series)**
by Susan Mayes and Sophy Tahta
(EDC Publications, 1995)

The Elements series
(Benchmark Books, 2000)

How the Internet Works
by P. Gralla
(Ziff-Davis Press, 1996)

**How? More Experiments
for the Young Scientist**
by Dave and Kathy Prochnow
(TAB Books, 1993)

Science Experiments series
(Benchmark Books, NY, 2001)

Sir Isaac Newton: His Life and Work
by E. N. Andrade
(Doubleday Anchor Books)

The Astronomers
by Colin A. Ronan
(Evans Brothers, 1964)

**Space Flight and Rocketry:
A Chronology**
(Facts on File, 1996)

The Story of Science series
(Benchmark Books, NY, 2000)

**The Victorian Internet:
The Remarkable Story of the
Telegraph and the Nineteenth
Century's On-Line Pioneers**
(Penguin Putnam Inc., 1999)

**When the
Sun Dies**
by Roy Gallant
(Marshall Cavendish,
1998)

**100 First-Prize Make-It-Yourself
Science Fair Projects**
(Sterling Publishing, 1999)

REFERENCE WORKS

Biographical Encyclopedia of Scientists
edited by Richard Olsen
(Marshall Cavendish, 1998)

The DK Science Encyclopedia
(DK Publishing Inc., 1998)

**Encyclopedia of Technology and
Applied Science**
(Marshall Cavendish, 2000)

The Kingfisher Science Encyclopedia
(Larousse Kingfisher Chambers, Inc., 2000)

The New Way Things Work
(Houghton Mifflin Company, 1998)

MAGAZINES

Astronomy
☎ (800) 533-6644
http://www.astronomy.com

Discover
☎ (800) 829-9132
http://www.discover.com

Explore Magazine
P.O. Box 37588
Boone, IA 50037-4588
☎ (877) 817-4395 toll free
http://www.exploremagazine.com

Muse
Smithsonian Institution
P.O. Box 7468
Red Oak, IA 51591-2468

Odyssey
Cousteau Society
930 W. 21st Street
Norfolk, VA 23517
☎ (804) 627-1144

Odyssey Magazine (online)
http://www.odysseymagazine.com

Science News
P.O. Box 1925
Marion, OH 43305
☎ (800) 552-4412

The Scientist
3535 Market Street
Suite 200
Philadelphia, PA 19104
☎ (215) 386-9601

INTERNET RESOURCES

Animation World Network
http://www.awn.com

Artificial Intelligence
http://www.aaai.org

Discovery Channel Network
http://dsc.discovery.com

European Space Agency
http://sci.esa.int

General: How Stuff Works
http://www.howstuffworks.com

Helicopters: Helicopter Association of America
http://www.rotor.com

Hubble Site
http://hubble.stsci.edu

National Aeronautics and Space Administration (NASA)
http://www.nasa.gov

JSC Imagery Services
http://images.jsc.nasa.gov

Lunar Prospector Mission
http://lunar.arc.nasa.gov

Science is Fun
http://scifun.chem.wisc.edu/scifun.html

Smithsonian Institution: Site for Kids
http://www.kidscastle.si.edu

Space Technology
http://www.space-technology.com

Technology Review Magazine
http://www.technologyreview.com

Television: early history
http://www.tvdawn.com

United States Environmental Protection Agency
http://www.epa.gov

Women in Physics
http://www.physics.ucla.edu

Glossary

abutment Structure that holds an arch in place.

acid rain Dilute sulfuric rain, which is found in rainwater and caused by polluting chemicals.

aileron (AY-luh-RAHN) Flaplike structure on the wing of an airplane.

airfoil A surface that causes air to move across it at different speeds, producing a lift force.

alkali (AL-kuh-ly) Compound that reacts with an acid to form a salt.

alloy A mixture of metals.

amphibious (am-FIB-ee-uhs) **vehicle** Vehicle able to travel over land and over water.

amplitude (AM-pluh-tood) The height of the peaks and troughs of a wave.

anemometer (AN-uh-MOM-uh-tur) An instrument for measuring the force or speed of the wind.

anesthetic (a-nuhz-THET-ik) A drug that causes a loss of sensation in a part of the body, or makes a patient become unconscious during an operation.

anthracite (AN-thruh-SYT) Hardest type of coal, which contains the most carbon.

antibiotic Drug that combats bacterial infection.

antibody A protein made from white blood cells that attacks foreign bodies in an immune response.

anticoagulant A chemical that prevents the blood from clotting.

antigen (ANT-i-juhn) A protein or carbohydrate on the surface of a foreign body that brings out an immune response.

aqueduct (AK-wuh-dukt) Bridge that carries water in a watertight trough.

aquifer Underground rocks containing water reserves.

artillery Weapons that fire missiles.

aseptic surgery Operations performed in sterile conditions to minimize the presence of microorganisms.

asphalt (AS-falt) A by-product of petroleum refining used on the surfaces of roads and sidewalks.

attrition (uh-TRI-shuhn) A chemical reaction between certain abrasives and the materials to be smoothed.

augur (AW-guhr) A corkscrew-shaped probe, which is used for drawing soil samples.

autopilot A system that steers ships, aircraft, and spacecraft automatically.

auxin A plant growth hormone.

automation Automatically controlled operation of a system by mechanical or electronic devices.

autopsy Examination of a corpse to determine the cause and the time of death.

axle Cylindrical bar on which a pair of wheels revolves.

ballast A heavy substance used to improve the stability and control of a ship or the ascent of a balloon.

ballistic trajectory (truh-JEK-tuh-ree) The curved path of an object such as a long-range missile.

balloon frame Internal wooden skeleton of a large building.

barometer (buh-RAM-uht-uhr) An instrument that measures the pressure of the atmosphere; used to assist in weather forecasting and for determining the altitude or the depth of both aircraft and submarines.

barrage (*energy production*) Artificial boom built across a tidal estuary.

base (*genetics*) One of the four chemical building blocks of DNA.

benign (*cancer*) Tumor that grows in one place without spreading.

binary code Information recorded as a 1 or 0.

biological control Introduction of natural enemies to limit the numbers of a pest population.

bit A single unit of binary data; can be either 0 or 1.

blanching Immersing food into steam or boiling water briefly.

boll The pod of a cotton plant.

bouquet (boo-KAY) The distinctive scent of a specific wine.

broadcasting (*farming*) Spreading seed or fertilizer over soil.

buoy A floating beacon moored to the sea or river bottom to mark a channel or submerged rocks.

byte A group of eight binary digits processed as a unit by a computer.

caffeine (ka-FEEN) A chemical that acts as a stimulant, found in beverages such as tea and coffee.

caisson (KAY-suhn) Waterfilled tank that carries a barge in a canal lift.

cantilever Trusses extending from piers that form a bridge when they are joined.

carbon dating Estimating the age of an object by measuring amounts of carbon-14, a radioactive isotope.

carburetor (KAR-buhr-rayt-uhr) Device that delivers the vaporized fuel-air mixture in an engine.

carcinogen (KAR-sin-uh-juhn) Agent that causes cancer.

catalyst Substance that speeds up a chemical reaction but which is not changed by that reaction.

cavitation The formation of tiny bubbles of gas, for example around the tops of hydrofoils.

cellulose (SEL-yuh-LOHS) Substance found in the walls of plant cells.

centrifuge (SEN-truh-fyooj) Device that spins objects or materials at very high speed to separate heavier substances from lighter ones.

chassis (CHA-see) Frame and working parts of a motor vehicle.

chemigation (kem-uh-GAY-shuhn) The injection of pesticides and fertilizers through irrigation systems.

chemotherapy (KEE-moh-ther-uh-pee) Using medicine to treat cancer.

chromosome (KROH-muh-som) The structure into which DNA is packed.

chronometer (kro-NAHM-uh-tuhr) An accurate timepiece that allowed mariners to figure out their longitudinal position.

circuit breaker Automatic switch that protects an electric circuit from overload.

cloning Producing offspring using a single cell of an adult organism.

clot Clumping of blood platelets.

cochineal (kahk-uh-NEEL) A red dye once made from crushed cochineal scale insects.

combustion A burning reaction.

compound Combination of two or more basic chemical substances.

compression (*computing*) Mathematical method of reducing the data included in an image.

compressive strength The ability of a material to resist a squeezing force.

conductor A material that transmits heat or electric current easily.

coniferous Trees with evergreen leaves, such as pines.

coppicing Cutting back trees at their base to harvest the shoots as poles.

coupler (*railroad*) A linking mechanism that joins separate railroad cars.

course Row or line of bricks in a wall or similar structure.

cracking (*oil industry*) Breaking long organic compounds in oil into smaller ones using catalysts.

critical mass Minimum amount of radioactive plutonium or uranium that can maintain a chain reaction of nuclear fission.

cryptogram (KRIP-tuh-gram) Message put into code.

current The flow of electrons through an electric circuit.

daub Mixture of twigs and straw with clay to make a building material that was common in the Middle Ages.

deflagration (DEF-luh-GRAY-shuhn) Combustion spreading outward with the burning substance setting fire to unburned chemical.

degrees of freedom (*robotics*) The number of directions in which a joint can move.

dehydration Removal of water from a substance.

delta wings Swept-back triangular wings used to reduce resistance on fighter aircraft and Concorde.

density The amount of mass relative to the volume of an object.

derailleur (di-RAY-luhr) Mechanism that shifts gears on a bicycle by moving the chain from one set of gears to another.

derrick A crane that employs a tackle, which is rigged at the end of a beam.

diode Electronic component that allows current to flow in one direction only.

DNA Molecules forming the genetic codes of all living organisms.

domestication To adapt, through selective breeding, an animal or plant to life with people.

doping (*electronics*) The addition of impurities to alter the properties of semiconducting materials.

downforce Downward force that pulls a fast-moving race car toward the road surface.

drag The resistance of air or water to the movement of objects.

drilling (*farming*) Poking seeds directly into the ground.

electrolysis (ih-lek-TRAH-luh-suhs) Breaking down substances by using electricity.

electrolyte (ih-LEK-trah-lyt) Liquid that allows electricity to flow through it.

electromagnet A core of magnetic material surrounded by a coil of wire through which a current passes to produce a powerful magnet.

electron Tiny particle that forms part of an atom.

electroplating Using one metal to coat another via electrolysis.

encryption Transforming a message into code.

enzyme (EN-zim) A protein that speeds up biological reactions.

epicenter The point of origin of an earthquake or earth tremor.

ergonomics (er-guh-NAM-iks) The science of designing objects so they can be used safely and efficiently.

escape velocity The speed that must be reached before a rocket launcher can escape from the pull of Earth's gravity.

fermenter Reactor that handles biochemical reactions.

filament A piece of wire through which a current passes, producing light and heat.

fission The splitting of the nucleus of an atom; this releases vast amounts of energy.

flail A free-swinging stick attached to a wooden handle that farmers once used to beat cereal crops; this separated the grain from the stalks.

flange A rim on the wheel of a wagon that kept it rolling along a groove in the track.

flashover Explosion in a fire when everything in a room or other confined space ignites at once.

flash point The temperature at which material catches fire.

fleece The coat of a wool-bearing animal, such as a sheep, goat, camel, or llama.

focal length The distance between the point of focus and the surface of a lens.

fodder Dried food such as hay, which is fed to farm animals.

font A set of letters, all in one style, used in book, newspaper, or magazine production.

fossil fuel A fuel, such as oil, coal, or natural gas, which is formed from the remains of long-dead plants and animals.

fractional distillation Process that separates out constituents of crude oil by their differing boiling points.

frequency The number of waves that pass a certain point in one second.

friction (FRIK-shuhn) The rubbing of different moving components, in an engine, for example, causing the production of heat.

fulcrum The support about which a balance or lever turns.

fusion The joining of nuclei to form heavier nuclei, with the release of huge quantities of energy; occurs in stars and some atomic bombs.

galvanization To coat iron or steel objects with zinc.

Geiger counter A device used to measure radioactivity.

gelatin Gel-like substance derived from animal tissues.

gene Combinations of bases which instruct cells how to make proteins, driving the development of a living organism.

generator A device that contains a rotating element that produces electrical energy.

genetic engineering Altering the genes of an organism.

geodetic (jee-uh-DET-ik) **surveying** Surveying the land while taking the curvature of earth into account.

geological trap A cap of rock or salt deposits that traps a reserve of oil or natural gas.

germination When seeds, such as cereal grains, begin to sprout shoots and roots.

ginning The process of removing seeds from cotton.

greenhouse effect A rise in global temperatures due to an increase in carbon dioxide in the atmosphere.

gridlock Traffic congestion.

hangar Covered storage area for airplanes at an airport or base.

hardware Components of a computer, such as the hard drive.

heliostat Mirror in a solar power station that focuses the light of the Sun onto a receiver.

hemostat An instrument used to compress a severed vein or artery.

herbicide A chemical that kills weeds and other plants.

homogenization (*farming*) Breaking up the fat globules found in milk into very fine particles.

hormone Biological messenger chemical; a product of living cells.

hull The main body of a ship or boat.

humus (HYOO-muhs) Partly decomposed animal or plant matter that forms part of the soil.

hydraulic (hy-DRAW-lik) **system** System driven by the property that fluids, such as oil or water, are resistant to compression.

hydrocarbon Molecule containing both hydrogen and carbon.

hydroelectricity Electric power produced by harnessing the movement of water in rivers and ocean tides.

hypocaust A Roman underfloor heating system with an underground furnace; a series of tile flues distributed the heat.

icebreaker Boat with a modified hull and powerful engines used to break through sea ice.

ignition (ig-NI-shuhn) Causing something to catch alight, such as diesel fuel in an engine.

inert A chemically unreactive element, such as xenon gas.

insulation Material that limits or halts the passage of heat, sound, or electrical current.

interference (*waves*) The product of the interaction of two or more light, sound, or any other types of waves.

interferon (in-TUHR-fir-ahn) Chemical produced by the body that makes white blood cells destroy cancer cells.

internal combustion engine An engine that burns fuel inside the cylinders that it contains.

irradiation (ir-AYD-ee-AY-shuhn) Exposure to radiation.

irrigation The process of bringing extra water to farmland.

isotope (EYE-suh-TOHPZ) Form of an element that is chemically the same as another form of the same element but having a slightly different mass.

keel A flat board attached to the hull of a boat that adds stability as the craft moves through the water.

kerosene Liquid fuel used to power the jet engines of aircraft.

kinetic (kuh-NET-ik) **energy** The energy of movement.

laminar flow Flow of air or water in smooth regular layers.

landfill A large hole in the ground into which trash is dumped.

latex Milky tree sap that is used to make rubber.

latitude Location measured as a distance either north or south of the equator.

lens A material that focuses light or other electromagnetic waves.

lift Forward and upward force produced by the shape of a wing that keeps an airplane airborne.

longitude Location measured either east or west around the globe from a fixed line.

loom A machine used for weaving fibers into cloth.

magnetron (MAG-nuh-TRAHN) A machine that generates pulses of radio waves in a radar installation.

malignant (*cancer*) Tumor that spreads through the body.

mass Amount of matter.

medium (*optics*) A material through which light passes.

methanol Clean-burning gasoline substitute produced from natural gas.

micrometeors Tiny pieces of rock floating through space.

microorganism Very small life-form.

monochromatic (MAHN-uh-kroh-MAT-ik) **light** Light of one wavelength and one color.

Morse code Combinations of dots and dashes used to spell out messages via telegraph wires.

mulching Adding a layer of decomposing plant material to soil to retain moisture, for insulation, or to increase nutrients.

nacre Chemical that forms the inside of a mollusk shell or pearls inside an oyster; also called mother-of-pearl.

neutron Particle without charge that forms part of a nucleus.

noise Unwanted deviations in or interference with an electrical signal.

novaculite (no-VAHK-yuh-lyt) A very hard fine-grained rock used to make whetstones, which sharpen metal blades.

nuclear fission Splitting an atomic nucleus to release energy.

nucleus Cluster of particles at the center of an atom.

nutrient Substance that provides nourishment to plants or to animals.

optical fiber Long, thin tube made of glass or plastic.

ore Rock that contains amounts of metals or of other minerals that are commercially viable.

organelle Subunit of a biological cell.

organic chemicals Any chemical compound that contains the element carbon.

organophosphate (or-guhn-no-FAHS-fayt) A chemical that contains both carbon and phosphorus; often used in pesticides and herbicides.

papyrus Paperlike material made from rushes; used in ancient Egypt as a writing material.

pasteurization Treating food rapidly to preserve it, using hot, dry heat.

pathogen (PATH-uh-juhn) An organism that causes disease in another organism.

payload The cargo carried by an aircraft or by a space vessel.

pedigree The recorded ancestry of a domesticated farm animal or of a domestic pet animal.

pesticide Chemical that kills pests such as insects, fungi, and weeds.

phagocyte (FAG-uh-syt) Cells in the blood that engulf and destroy foreign bodies.

photon (FO-tahn) A particle that forms light.

photovoltaic (fo-to-vahl-TAY-ik) **effect** Property of certain compounds that produce electrical current when exposed to light.

piezoelectric (pee-AY-zoh-uh-LEK-trik) **effect** The production of electricity in response to pressure; occurs in minerals including tourmaline and quartz.

pixels Tiny dots of color that together form an image on a computer or TV screen.

plane (*boats*) To skim across the surface of the water.

pneumatic (noo-MAT-ik) **system** A system driven by compressed air.

polymer (PAH-luh-muhr) A chemical compound consisting of a long chain of repeating units.

pozzolana (pot-zo-LAH-nah) Volcanic ash used by the Romans to make concrete.

precipitation A deposit on the ground of hail, mist, rain, sleet, or snow.

protein Chemicals called amino acids linked together in chains.

proton Positively charged particle that forms part of a nucleus.

prototype The first full-sized working version of a new type or design of a vehicle.

puddle Waterproof putty once used to line canals.

quarantine (KWOR-uhn-teen) Keeping infected or potentially infected disease carriers in isolation.

radiology The use of radioactivity to diagnose and treat disease.

rayon Artificial fiber, which is made to resemble silk, and is produced from cellulose.

reagent Chemical that takes part in a reaction.

refraction The deflection of light when passing from one medium to another medium.

relative humidity The amount of moisture in the air.

retina (RET-uh-nuh) A sensory membrane lining the back of the eyeball that receives the image from the lens, converting it to electrical signals that pass to the brain.

rifling Spiral grooves inside the barrel of a gun.

rudder Curved board used to steer a ship or boat.

scaffolding Skeleton of metal and/or wood, which is built around a building to give access during construction or repairs.

scalpel A small, thin-bladed knife used in surgery.

scythe A tool used to mow cereals and other grasses; consists of a long curving blade fastened to a long wooden handle.

seismographs Mechanical devices used to measure and record the strength and epicenter of an earthquake or earth tremor.

sequencer Device used to identify the components of proteins.

semaphore A system of visual signals involving the movement of a pair of flags, one in each hand.

semiconductor Material which conducts electrical current poorly when pure but which allows much more current through it when impurities are added.

sextant A navigation device once used to measure the position of the sun.

silage Grass and hay fermented in a silo to produce a succulent winter food for livestock.

smog An airborne mixture of fog and polluting chemicals.

software Computer program, often saved on a floppy disk or CD-ROM.

soldering Method of joining metals.

solenoid A coil of wire which, when carrying a current, acts like a magnet; often used as switches and controls for mechanical devices.

solvent A liquid that can dissolve other compounds.

sphygmomanometer (sfig-mo-muh-NAHM-uh-tuhr) An instrument used by physicians to measure blood pressure.

spinneret A small metal plate with fine holes through which chemicals are forced in the spinning of synthetic fibers, such as nylon.

spoil Soil and rock removed by excavation or dredging.

stealth airplane Aircraft designed to be almost invisible to radar.

stethoscope (STETH-uh-SKOPH) An instrument used to study sounds produced by the body.

stevedore A worker who loads and unloads ships in a port.

streamlined The shape of an object, such as an automobile or airplane, that is designed to minimize drag.

supersonic Any airplane or other craft that is capable of moving faster than the speed of sound in air.

surfactant Active cleansing ingredient in soap and in detergent.

synthesize To manufacture any product artificially, often one that occurs naturally in a similar form.

synthetic An artificially manufactured product, often one that occurs naturally in a similar form.

tandem A bicycle that is designed to be ridden by two riders simultaneously.

telegraph Communications system in which messages pass along copper wires in the form of electrical pulses.

tensile strength The ability of a material to resist a stretching force.

theodolite (the-AH-duh-lyt) A device that is used by surveyors to measure angles of buildings and other objects accurately.

thermal efficiency The percentage of heat produced by a power station that is converted into electricity.

thermocouple A device used to measure temperature that records voltage between two different types of metal.

thermometer An instrument for measuring temperature using a liquid that rises and falls with temperature.

thermoplastic A plastic that softens when heated.

thermoplastic adhesive A plastic adhesive that forms a strong bond but softens when heated.

thermosetting adhesive A plastic adhesive that hardens when heated.

thermosetting plastic A plastic that hardens when heated.

thermostat A device used to regulate temperature automatically.

throttle The valve that controls the fuel-air mixture, which enters an engine.

thrust Forward-acting force provided by the engines of an airplane or of a rocket launcher.

tiller Lever used to control the angle of a rudder on a boat.

torque (TORK) A force that produces a rotation.

toxicity A measure of how poisonous a chemical is.

trace element Element needed in tiny quantities by organisms.

transgenic Organism that contains a gene from another species.

tread A series of patterns on a tire that aid grip.

triangulation Mathematical technique used by surveyors to figure out the positions of different objects.

tyrian (TYR-ee-uhn) **purple** A dye made from certain shellfish.

ultraviolet light Invisible light of a high wavelength.

undercarriage Wheels and landing gear located on the underside of an airplane.

vacuum A space completely devoid of matter, such as deep space.

velocity The speed of an object in a specific direction.

veneer (vuh-NIR) A thin layer of (usually decorative) wood covering an object.

virus Tiny living agent that causes diseases.

viscosity A measure of the stickiness of water or air.

vortex generator Device added to an airplane wing to prevent stalling.

vulcanization A process of altering rubber to make it stronger and to help it keep its shape.

wavelength The distance between two adjacent peaks of a wave, such as a light beam, tidal wave, or a sound wave.

zeppelin Giant airship used for civil and military aviation; made in Germany between 1900 and 1936.

zoonosis Any disease that can pass between humans and animals, such as bubonic plague.

Subject Indexes

AGRICULTURE AND FOOD

Agriculture **1:20–21**
  birth of **9**:710
  farm storage **4**:261
  fertilizers **1**:*21*;
      4:**264–265**; **7**:551
  sustainable farming **7**:519
  see also crops; horticulture,
      livestock farming; pest
      control
ammonia, and fertilizers
      4:265
animal breeding **1:36**
  selective breeding **1**:36;
      3:188
  see also livestock farming
animals, treatment of *see*
      veterinary medicine
animal transportation
      1:37–38; **9**:*649*
aphids **2**:*84*; **7**:*528*
aquaculture **1:48–49**
  see also fishing industry
aquifers **5**:385
auxins **5**:351

Bacillus thuringiensis **2**:85
bacteria, for biological
      control **2**:85
baking industry **1:64–65**
beer **2**:88, 89, 90, *98–99*
beverages **1:72–75**; **2**:88;
      4:289
  beer **2:88**, 89, 90, *98–99*
  cocoa **1**:73
  coffee **1**:72–73, *75*; **4**:289

fruit juices **1**:75
  spirits **1**:74–75
  tea **1**:72; **3**:*184*
  wine **1**:*73–74*
biological control **2:84–85**
  see also crop farming
Birdseye, Clarence **4**:289
blackfly, citrus **3**:187
blanching, food **4**:288, 291
bourbon **1**:75
bovine growth hormone
      (BST) **3**:188
brandy **1**:75
bread, making **1**:*64–65*
breeding, animal
  see animal breeding
  plant **5**:349–350
brewing industry **2:98–99**
BSE (mad cow disease)
      6:412
BST (bovine growth
      hormone) **3**:188
bucket wheels **5**:386

Cakes and cookies **1**:65
canning **4**:289
carbohydrates **4**:294
carrots **7**:519
Carson, Rachel **7**:528
cattle **6**:*412*
  dairy **3**:188–*189*; **6**:412
cheese **3**:189; **4**:*292*
chemigation **3**:187
chickens **6**:413
cocoa **1**:73
coffee **1**:72–73, 75; **4**:289
combine harvesters
      5:*332–333*; **6**:428

companion planting **7**:519,
      527
cookies **1**:*65*
coppicing **4**:299–300
crabs, fishing for **4**:280–281
crawlers **10**:750, 751
crops
  cash **3**:184
  farming **3:184–185**;
      5:351; **9**:654
  genetically-engineered
      4:314–315; **7**:529
  irrigation **5:384–387**;
      10:778
  rotation **7**:519
  spraying **3:186–187**
  storage **4**:261
  see also agriculture;
      fertilizers; harvesting
      machinery; pesticide
      and herbicide;
      horticulture; plows;
      tractors
cultivators (harrows) **3**:184
cuttings, plant **5**:351

Dairy industry **3:188–189**
  see also livestock farming
DDT **3**:187; **7**:528, 529
deforestation **4**:301
distillation, of spirits **1**:74
drainage, land **5**:387
drilling, seeds **3**:184
drinks *see* beverages
drying, food **4**:289

Erosion, soil **9**:654
ethylene **5**:351

Farming *see* agriculture
farm storage **4:261**
fat(s), processing **4**:291–292
fermentation
  and baking **1**:64, 65
  and wine making **1**:73, 74
fertilizers **1**:*21*; **4:264–265**;
      7:551
fish
  farming *see* aquaculture
  stocks **4**:281
fishing industry **4:278–281**
flails **5**:332
flowers, growing **5**:*348*, 349
food
  additives **4**:293
  genetically modified **4**:315
food preservation
      4:288–289
fish and shellfish **4**:281
food technology **2**:90;
      4:290–294
  see also baking industry;
      beverages; brewing;
      food preservation
forestry **4:299–301**
freeze-drying **4**:289
freezers **8**:596
freezing, food **4**:289
fruit
  growing **5**:348–349
  harvesting **5**:333
  processing **4**:*288–289*
fruit juices **1**:75

Gin **1**:75
gluten **1**:64
glycophosphates **7**:528
grafting, plants **5**:351
grain
  elevators **4**:*261*
  harvesting **5**:333
  storage **4**:261
  see also crop farming

Harrows (cultivators) 3:184
harvesting machinery 5:332–333
hay 4:261
herbicides *see* pesticides and herbicides
hoppers 3:184
hormones, plant 1:20; 5:351
horticulture 5:348–351
 see also agriculture
Howard, Albert 7:518
Hussey, Obed 9:713
hybridization 5:350
hydroponics 5:350

Inbreeding 1:36
insecticides *see* pesticides and herbicides
insemination, artificial 6:412
integrated pest management (IPM) 3:187; 7:529
IPM (integrated pest management) 3:187; 7:529
irradiation, food 4:289; 7:497
irrigation 5:384–387; 10:778
 chemigation 3:187

Lactic acid 3:189
ladybugs 2:84
lager 2:99
legumes 3:185
livestock farming 1:21; 6:412–413
 cloning and 2:149
 veterinary medicine and 10:763, 764
lobsters, fishing for 4:281

McCormick, Cyrus 6:428; 9:713
mad cow disease (BSE) 6:412; 10:765

manure 4:264, 265
meat, processing 4:290
milk 3:188–189
milling 1:64
moths, gypsy 2:84
mulching 7:519

Nematicides 7:528
nicotine 7:527
nitrogen, in the soil 3:185; 4:264

Oils, processing 4:291–292
organic farming 7:518–519
organophosphates 7:528
outbreeding 1:36
oysters 1:49

Paddy fields 5:384, 387
parasitoids 2:84–85
pasteurization 3:189; 4:288
pearls 1:49
Persian wheels 5:386
pest control 1:20–21
 biological control 2:84–85
 see also pesticides and herbicides
pesticides and herbicides 1:21; 3:185, 186–187; 7:527–529
 pollution from 7:529, 550–551
pheromones 3:187
phosphorus, in fertilizers 4:265
pigs 6:413
planting, companion 7:519, 527
plants
 breeding 5:349–350
 cuttings 5:351
 grafting 5:351
 growing from seeds 5:350
 hormones 1:20; 5:351
plowing 3:184
 contour 1:20
plows 7:547
pollarding 4:299–300

pollination 5:349–350
potassium, in fertilizers 4:265
poultry 6:413
proteins 4:292
pumps 8:575
pyrethrum 7:528

Reaping machines 9:713
refrigeration 8:595–596
 of crops 4:261
 of food 4:288–289
rennin 3:189
reservoirs 5:384
rice 3:184; 5:384, 387
rubber 8:616–617; 10:746

Salting, food 4:289
sawmills 4:300
screwworms, biological control of 2:85
scythes 5:330, 332, 333
seaweed 1:48
seeds
 growing plants from 5:350
 sowing 3:184
shadufs 5:384, 386
sheep 6:413
 cloning 2:148–149
 dipping 1:47
shellfish, aquaculture 1:49
sickles 5:332, 333
silage 4:261; 5:333
Silent Spring (book) 7:528

slash-and-burn agriculture 4:300
snails, biological control 2:85
soil, nitrogen 3:185; 4:264
soil science 9:654
solid sets 5:386
sowing 3:184
soy foods 4:294
spirits 1:74–75
sprinklers 5:384, 386–387
Steiner, Rudolf 7:518
sterilization, of food 4:288
subsoilers 3:184
sugar, processing 4:292–293, 294
sugarcane, fuel from 4:305
sugaring, food 4:289

Tea 1:72
 plantations 3:184
terraces, farming on 3:185
threshing 5:332
tillage 3:184
toads, cane 2:85
tomatoes 4:315
tracked vehicles, for farming 10:750, 751
tractors (farming) 7:502; 10:751–752

Cell phones are based on overlapping cells, each with a transceiver (transmitter-receiver).

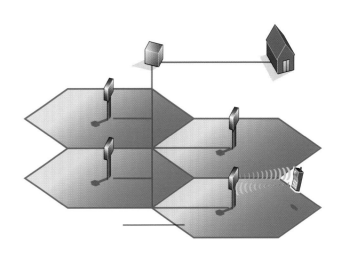

transgenic organisms
4:315–*316*

trees
  coppicing 4: 299–300
  rubber 8:*616*, 617
  see also forestry

triazines 7:528

Veal 6:412

vegetables
  harvesting 5:333
  processing 4:288–289
  see also horticulture

veterinary medicine
  10:763–765

vitamins 4:293

viticulture 1:73

Wasps, parasitic 2:84–85;
  3:187

water hyacinths 2:84

wheat 1:64

whiskey 1:74–75

wine 1:*73–74*

winnowing 5:332

Yeast, and baking 1:64–65

ENGINEERING
AND
CONSTRUCTION

Abrasives 1:12–13

absolute temperature scale
  10:741–742

absolute zero 8:596; 10:742

AC *see* alternating current

acceleration, due to gravity
  6:431

Acheson, Edward Goodrich
  1:12

acoustics 1:14–15

adhesives 1:16

aeolipiles 9:685

aerodynamics 1:17–19

air conditioning 1:22–23
  see also heating systems

airports and airfields
  1:31–33; 2:143

airport surveillance radar
  (ASR) 8:579

Akashi-Kaikyo Bridge
  2:107

alpha particles and alpha
  decay 7:497;
  8:580–581

alternating current (AC)
  3:213, 218, 219–220

AC generators 3:*221*

AC motors 3:221–222

alternators 3:222

ammonium nitrate-fuel oil
  mixtures (ANFOs)
  4:258

Ampère, André-Marie
  6:419

anemometers 6:450–*451*

ANFOs (ammonium
  nitrate-fuel oil
  mixtures) 4:258

APMs (automated people
  movers) 8:607

aqueducts 2:*104*, 116

archeology 1:50–51

asphalt 8:602, 603

Aspidin, Joseph 2:127

ASR (airport surveillance
  radar) 8:579

Aswan Dam 5:*358*

attrition 1:12

automated people movers
  (APMs) 8:607

Babbitt metal 6:430

backhoes 3:179, *180*

bagpipes 7:*487*

balances 10:*786–787*

balloon framing 2:108

bassoons 7:488

batteries 1:70–71;
  3:213–214; 5:362

beams, cantilever
  9:646–647

bearings 4:262; 6:430

Becquerel, Henri 7:497

beta particles and beta
  decay 1:70; 7:497;
  8:581

bimetallic strips 10:742

biomedical engineering
  (bionics) 2:86–87;
  4:255

bolts 4:263

breakwaters 2:143

bricks and masonry
  2:100–101, 109, *110*

bridges 2:102–107
  Akashi-Kaikyo Bridge
    2:107
  arch 2:*103*, 104–105;
    4:*254*
  beam 2:*103*–104
  bridging tanks 10:750
  cable-stayed 2:107
  cantilever 2:*103*, 105–106
  cement and concrete
    2:102-103
  clapper 2:103
  Confederation Bridge
    2:107
  moveable 2:107
  pontoon 2:103
  Seto-Ohashi Bridge 2:107
  suspension 2:*103*, 106,
    107, 112
  Tacoma Narrows 1:18;
    2:106
  Tay Bridge disaster 2:106
  truss 2:104

Brindley, James 2:143

Broglie, prince Louis de
  6:459

Bronze Age 9:710

Brooklyn Bridge 2:106

brownouts 3:217

Brunel, Isambard Kingdom
  2:110, 143, 144; 9:698

Brunelleschi, Filippo 2:110

buildings
  aerodynamics and 1:19
  demolition 3:*196*–197

building techniques
  2:108–112

foundations 4:302
  see also bricks and
    masonry; skyscrapers

bulldozers 3:179, 180

butterfly effect 2:132

Cables, electrical 2:**114**

caissons 4:302; 6:409

canals
  building 2:115–116
  Panama Canal 2:116, 118
  Suez Canal 3:208

capacitors 3:*216*, 217; 6:455

Cape Canaveral, demolition
  at 3:197

carbon, isotopes 7:496, 497

carbon fiber 1:76

carborundum 1:12

cathedrals, Gothic 2:*109*,
  110

"cat's eyes" 8:602

cells, battery 1:70–71

Celsius temperature scale
  10:741

cement and concrete 2:101,
  111–112, **126–127**
  for bridges 2:102–103
  prestressed concrete 2:127
  reinforced concrete 2:102,
    103, *111*, 127; 4:302

roads 8:602

central heating 5:339–341

ceramics, abrasive 1:13

cesium atomic clocks
  10:745

chain reaction **7**:498–499, 500–501

Channel Tunnel **5**:329; **10**:757

chaos theory **2**:132

Chernobyl disaster **2**:144; **7**:*498*, 548

chimneys, factory, demolition **3**:197

circuit breakers **3**:218

civil engineering **2**:142–145; **4**:252–*253*, 254

  railroad construction **8**:589–591

  roads **8**:600–605

  see also bridges; foundations; skyscrapers; surveying; tunnels

clarinets **7**:487, 488

clay **2**:100

clocks and watches **10**:743–*745*

  atomic clocks **5**:329; **10**:*745*

  digital **3**:*206*; **10**:*745*

  electric **10**:744–745

  mechanical **10**:*744*

coastal engineering **2**:143

color **3**:164–165

Colosseum **2**:111–112, *127*

combustion **4**:257, 303–304

compactors **3**:179

concrete *see* cement and concrete

conduction (heat) **5**:338, 339, 368

conductors, electrical **3**:213

Confederation Bridge **2**:107

Congreve, William **6**:466

construction sites **3**:178–180

convection **5**:338, 339

corrosion **3**:182

cranes **3**:183; **7**:554

crawlers **10**:748, 750, 751

creosote **7**:521

Crookes, William **8**:583

cryogenics **8**:596

Crystal Palace **2**:110–111

Dams **2**:*145*; **3**:190–191; **5**:*358*–359; **10**:*776*, *781*

Darrieus turbines **10**:759

Davy, Sir Humphry **3**:*225*; **6**:410–411

DC *see* direct current

deflagration **4**:257

demolition **3**:196–197

detonation **4**:257

diamonds **1**:12, *13*

  synthetic **1**:12, 13

diffraction **10**:783

diggers **10**:*750*

dikes **2**:143; **3**:191

direct current (DC) **3**:218, 219

DC generators **3**:*221*

DC motors **3**:*220*, 221

discharge tubes, fluorescent **6**:411

distance, measured using lasers **5**:391

domes **4**:*255*

drag **1**:17

drawbridges **2**:107

dredging **3**:208–209

drums **7**:489

duplexers **8**:578

dynamite **4**:258

dynamos **3**:222

Earthquakes, and seismography **6**:461; **7**:505; **8**:631

eddy currents **3**:222

Edison, Thomas Alva **3**:230; **6**:411, 474; **9**:658, 686, 712; **10**:735

EDMs (electronic distance measuring devices) **9**:708

EIAs (environmental impact assessments) **2**:145

Eiffel Tower **2**:111

electricity **3**:212–214

  transmission **3**:215–218

electric circuits **3**:213–214, 231

electric current **3**:213–*214*, 230–231; **6**:445

  static **3**:213

electric motors **3**:219–222; **6**:420

  synchronous **10**:744–745

electrodes **1**:70

electrolytes **1**:70–71

electromagnetic force **3**:212

electromagnets **3**:221, *226*–227; **6**:418

  in loudspeakers **6**:*455*

  in televisions **6**:420; **10**:733

electromechanical devices **3**:226–228

electronic distance measuring devices (EDMs) **9**:708

electrons

  and atom **7**:496

  and batteries **1**:71

  and electricity **3**:212–213, 214

  and electrolysis **3**:224

  and light particles (photons) **5**:389

electron tubes **3**:234–235

elevators (lifts) **2**:111; **3**:236–237; **9**:646

  grain **4**:*261*

Empire State Building **9**:*646*, 647

enamel, vitreous **7**:521

engineering **4**:252–255

  aerospace **4**:253

  biomedical (bionics) **2**:86–87; **4**:255

  chemical **2**:134–136; **4**:253

  civil *see* civil engineering

  coastal **2**:143

  electrical and electronics **4**:255

  environmental **2**:144; **4**:254

  genetic **1**:36; **2**:89; **4**:314–316; **7**:529

  marine **6**:421–423

  mechanical **6**:426–428

  military **4**:253

  nuclear **4**:254–255

environmental engineering **2**:144; **4**:254

environmental impact assessments (EIAs) **2**:145

erosion, coastal **2**:143

Evinrude, Ole **8**:564

excavators **3**:*178*–180; **5**:356; **6**:462

  draglines **6**:463

explosives **4**:257–258

  for demolition **3**:197

A radio antenna's signal can be increased, while a radio receiver's design determines the waves it is sensitive to.

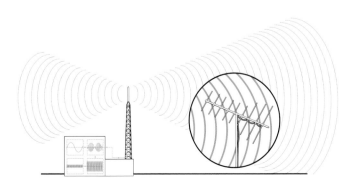

Faraday, Michael **3**:225; **8**:582

Farenheit temperature scale **10**:741

fastening and joining **4:262–263**

FEDs (field emission displays) **3**:235

feet (units of measurement) **6**:425

fiberglass **5**:*368*

field emission displays (FEDs) **3**:235

field-emission microscopes (FEMs) **6**:459

fires, open **5**:339

fission, nuclear **4**:247; **7**:498, 500

flashlights **3**:213–214; **7**:540

flood barriers **3**:191

Florence, cathedral **2**:110

flying buttresses **2**:109

forces, and movement **6**:431–432

formwork **2**:109

foundations **4:302**

Francis turbines **10**:759, 776

freezers **8**:596

Frisch, Otto **7**:499

fuel cells **1**:71

fulcrums **6**:*432*

fusion, nuclear **4**:247; **7**:498, 499

Gallons **6**:425

Galvani, Luigi **3**:224–225

gamma rays **7**:497; **8**:581
   telescopes **10**:730

gas turbines and engines **4:310–311**; **6**:422
   helicopter **5**:344

gears **4:312–313**; **6**:433
   bicycle **1**:76–77, *78*; **6**:430
   in clocks **10**:744

generators, electric **3**:219, 222; **6**:420

Giffard, Henri **1**:30, 67

Gilbert, William **6**:418

glues **4**:262–263; **10**:798

Goddard, Robert **6**:466; **8**:*612*–613

graders **3**:179

Grand Coulee Dam **5**:359

gravity, acceleration due to **6**:431

Great Britain (ship) **2**:144

Great Eastern (ship) **2**:144

Great Exhibition (1851) **2**:110–111

Greathead, James Henry **9**:698

Great Pyramid of Khufu **2**:110

Great Wall of China **2**:*142*

grids, power **3**:215
   see also electricity

gum arabic **1**:16

gunpowder **4**:257

Gunter's chain **9**:707

gypsum **2**:127

Hahn, Otto **7**:499

Hale, William **8**:611

hardness, Mohs' scale of **1**:13

harps **7**:488

heat exchangers **1**:23; **5:337**, 341

heating systems **5:338–341**
   heat pumps **5**:341

Hertz, Heinrich **8**:583; **10**:734

Hong Kong
   airport **1**:*32*
   Bionic Tower **9**:647
   Cross-Harbor Tunnel **10**:757

Hooke, Robert **6**:459; **10**:744

Hoover Dam **3**:*190*, 191

humidity, measuring **6**:431

Huygens, Christiaan **9**:685; **10**:743, 783

hydraulics **5:356–357**
   brakes **2**:96–97; **5**:*357*
   on excavators **3**:178; **5**:356
   robotic arms **8**:608–609
   shock absorbers **1**:63
   tractor systems **10**:752

hygrometers **6**:451

hypocausts **5**:*340*

Impedance **3**:217

inches **6**:425

induction, electrostatic **3**:213

inductors **3**:217, *218*, 231

inertia **6**:432

infrared radiation, telescopes **10**:730

instruments, musical *see* musical instruments

insulation **5:368**
   acoustic **5**:368
   electrical **3**:213; **5**:368
   thermal **5**:368

integrated circuits (silicon chips; microchips) **3**:172, *174*, 231, *232*; **5:369–370**; **8**:633
   manufacture **3**:232; **5**:369–*370*
   PLCs **3**:228

interference **10**:783

ions, positive and negative **7**:497

Iron Age **9**:711

isobars and isotherms **6**:451

isotopes **7**:496–497

Itaipu Dam **2**:*145*

Japan, bridges **2**:107

jetties **7**:553

joints (mechanical) **4**:262

Kelvin temperature scale **10**:741–742

Kettering, Charles **6**:466

kettledrums **7**:489

keyboards, electronic **7**:*489*

kieselgurh **4**:258

kilns **2**:100

kilowatt-hours **3**:218

Lacquer **7**:521

Laerdal Tunnel **10**:757

laminar flow **1**:17

landscaping, hard **3**:178–179

Leclanché, Georges **1**:70

Leeuwenhoek, Antonie van **6**:459

Lesseps, Ferdinand de **2**:116, 118

levees **3**:191

levers **6**:*432*, 433

lightbulbs **3**:*230*; **6**:*411*

lighthouses, construction **6**:409

lighting **6:410–411**

limestone, for cement **2**:101, *126*, 127

loaders **3**:180

lodestones **6**:418
   see also compasses

Lorenz, Edward **2**:132

lute family **7**:488–489

lyres **7**:488

Magnetometers **1**:50

magnetrons **8**:578; **9**:691

magnets and magnetism **6:418–420**
   in motors **3**:*220*–221

mantles, gas **6**:410

Marconi, Guglielmo **8**:583; **9**:713, 716; **10**:734–735, *793*, 794, 795

marine engineering **6:421–423**

mass
   and radiation **7**:497–498
   and weight **10**:786

Volume numbers are in **boldface type** followed by colons. Page numbers in **boldface type** refer to main articles and their illustrations; page numbers in *italic type* refer to picture captions.

Maxwell, James Clerk **8**:582–583

measurement **6**:425

mechanical advantage **6**:*433*

mechanical engineering **4**:254; **6**:*426–428*

mechanical transmission **6**:*429–430*
  automobiles **1**:57; **4**:*313*; **5**:357; **6**:*429*–430
  motorcycles **6**:472

mechanics **6**:431–433

mechatronics **6**:427

Meitner, Lise **7**:499

meteorological instruments **6**:450–451

meters (units of measurement) **6**:425

microchips *see* integrated circuits

microscopy **6**:406, 438, 439, **456–459**

miles **6**:425

Mohs' scale of hardness **1**:13

mortar **2**:101, 109, 110

motion
  linear **6**:431
  Newton's laws of **6**:431–432

motors
  electric *see* electric motors
  outboard and inboard **6**:422

moviemaking **6**:473–478

musical instruments **1**:15; **7**:486–489

Nails **4**:*262*

Newcomen, Thomas **6**:427; **9**:685–686

Newton, Isaac **6**:432

Nipkow, Paul **10**:735, *736*

Nipkow disks **10**:735, *736*

NIST-F1 (clock) **10**:*745*

nitroglycerin **4**:258

Nobel, Alfred **4**:258

nuclear quadrupole resonance **1**:50

Oberth, Hermann **8**:613

oboes **7**:488

Ohain, Hans von **6**:428

organs (musical instruments) **7**:489

Orsted, Hans Christian **6**:419

Otis, Elisha Graves **2**:111; **3**:237; **9**:646

Paints and surface coatings **7**:520–521
  mixing **3**:*165*

Panama Canal **2**:116, 118

Papin, Denis **9**:685

Parsons, Charles **9**:687

Pelton wheels **10**:758–*759*, 776

percussion instruments **7**:487, 489

photomasking **3**:*230*, 232

phthalocyanines **7**:520

pianos **7**:*488*, 489

piers **7**:553

piezoelectric effect **6**:455

pile drivers **4**:302

piles **4**:302

pivots **4**:262

pneumatics **5**:357
  for robotic arms **8**:609

polders **2**:143

polishes **7**:521

Pompidou Center, Paris **4**:*253*

ports **2**:143; **7**:552–555

potential difference **3**:214

pounds (units of measurement) **6**:425

powder coatings **7**:521

power lines **3**:*214*
  accessing the Internet via **3**:167

power take off shafts **10**:752

pozzolana **2**:111–112

precipitators, electrostatic **1**:22

prime movers **3**:222

prototypes **4**:252; **6**:425

puddle **2**:115–116

pulleys **6**:*433*

pumps **8**:575

pylons, electricity **3**:*215*

pyramids, Egyptian **2**:110; **9**:709

Pythagoras, and music **7**:486

Quartz, in clocks **10**:745

Radar **8**:578–579
  airport surveillance (ASR) **8**:579
  archeology and **1**:50
  radiation (heat) **5**:338, 339, 368
  radiation (ionizing) **7**:497; **8**:580–581
  radiators, heat exchangers and **5**:337
  radioactive waste **5**:*334*
  radioactivity **7**:496–497
  radiocarbon dating **1**:51; **7**:497
  radioisotopes **7**:497
  radiosondes **6**:451
  radio telescopes **10**:729–730
  railroads, construction **8**:589–591
  rain gauges **6**:*450*, 451
  ramps **6**:433
  rarefaction **10**:782
  RDX **4**:258
  reed beds **2**:145
  refrigeration **8**:595–596
    and air-conditioning systems **1**:23
    heat exchangers and **5**:337, 341

relays **3**:*228*

reed **3**:227

reservoirs **3**:190, 191; **5**:358–359, 384

resistance, electrical **3**:214

resistors **3**:217, 231, *233*

Richter scale **8**:631

rivets **4**:262

roads **8**:600–605
  and the environment **2**:145

Roebling, John and Washington **2**:106

Romans, ancient **9**:711
  cement and concrete **2**:111–112, 126
  civil engineering **2**:142
  glass **9**:*711*

rooms, "clean" **1**:22

rust **3**:182

Rutherford, Ernest **7**:497

Sandblasting **1**:*12*, 13

satellites, for surveying **9**:*709*

saxophones **7**:487, 488

scaffolding **2**:109

scales, electronic **10**:*787*

scanning electron microscopes (SEMs) **6**:*457*, 458

scanning tunneling microscopes (STMs) **6**:459

scrapers **3**:179

Gas enters a simple engine through the lower valve. Heat, applied from the top of the engine, causes the gas in the cylinder to expand.

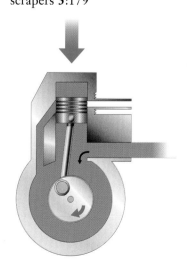

screws **4**:263

sealants **7**:521

Seikan Tunnel **10**:757

seismograms **8**:631

seismographs **8**:631

seismography **6**:461; **7**:505; **8:631**

SEMs (scanning electron microscopes) **6**:*457*, 458

Seneca, Lucius **6**:459

Seto-Ohashi Bridge **2**:107

shot blasting **1**:13

silicon carbide (carborundum) **1**:12

silicon chips *see* integrated circuits

S.I. units **6**:425

skyscrapers **2**:111; **5**:*378*; **9:646–647**

slide bars **4**:262

Smeaton, John **2**:126–127, 143

soil, archeology and **1**:51

soldering **4**:263

solenoids **3**:227–228

sonar **1**:*15*

archeology and **1**:50

sound

and Doppler effect **8**:579

and electricity **6**:453

frequency **8**:579

speed **10**:783

study of *see* acoustics

soundproofing **5**:368

South Fork Dam **3**:191

space frames **2**:112

speed **6**:431

Sperry, Elmer **6**:466

spoil

from dredging **3**:209

removal **3**:178

steelyards **10**:786

Stevens, John F. **2**:116

Stevenson screens **6**:451

STMs (scanning tunneling microscopes) **6**:459

stone, building in **2**:110

Stone Age **9**:710

stopcocks **10**:762

strips, metallic **10**:742

substations, electrical **3**:218

Suez Canal **3**:208

sundials **10**:*743*

surface coatings **7**:521

surfactants **7**:521

surveying **9:707–709**

Swan, Joseph **9**:712

synthesizers **7**:487

Tacoma Narrows Bridge **1**:18; **2**:106

tambourines **7**:489

tape measures **9**:707

Tay Bridge disaster **2**:106

technology, history of **9:710–713**

telescopes **10:728–730**

Telford, Thomas **2**:143

temperature, measurement *see* thermography and thermometry

Thames Barrier **10**:762, *778*

theodolites **9**:*707*, *708*

thermocouples **6**:450; **10**:742

thermography **10**:742

thermometry **6**:450; **10:741–742**

thermos bottles **5**:368

time **10:743–745**

TNT (trinitrotoluene) **4**:258

toasters **3**:227–228

toothpaste **1**:12, 13

torque **3**:221; **5**:342

total stations (surveying) **9**:708–709

transducers **6**:453; **10**:725, **753**

transformers **3**:217–218, 232

transits **9**:708

Trans-Ko'Olau Tunnel **10**:757

transmission, mechanical *see* mechanical transmission

transmission electron microscopes (TEMs) **6**:*457*, 458

Trevithick, Richard **8**:587; **9**:686

triangulation **9**:707, 708, 709

trinitrotoluene (TNT) **4**:258

trombones **7**:488

trucks

construction trucks **10**:755

dump **3**:180; **5**:*357*; **10**:755

weighing **10**:787

trusses **4**:262

tumbling mills **1**:13

tunnels **10:756–757**

canals **2**:116

construction **5**:329; **6**:427, *428*; **9**:698–700

GPS **5**:329

turbines **10:758–759**

gas *see* gas turbines and engines

reaction and impulse **10**:758

steam **3**:236; **6**:421; **8**:567, 568; **9**:684, *687*; **10**:759

water **5**:358, *359*; **8**:*566*; **10:758–759**, 776

wind **10**:759, 790, 791, *792*

Ultrasound **1**:15

ultraviolet light **3**:*164*; **6**:*411*

telescopes **10**:730

Vaiont Dam **3**:191

valves **10:761–762**

varnishes **7**:521

vaults (arches) **2**:109

ventilation systems **1**:19

subway **9**:*699*, 701

Volta, Alessandro **3**:224–225

voltage **3**:214

voltaic piles **3**:225

von Braun, Wernher **8**:613, 615

Walls

cavity **2**:*101*

dry-stone **2**:110

watches **10**:743–*744*, 745

Watson-Watt, Robert **8**:578

Watt, James **9**:686, 687

watts **3**:218

wave motion **10:782–783**

weather, forecasting **6**:451; **8**:*622*

weigh bridges **10**:787

weights and measures **10:786–787**

see also measurement

welding **4**:263

Westinghouse, George **9**:687

wheels **6**:433; **9**:710

see also tire **10**:746

Whittle, Frank **6**:*427*, 428

windmills **10**:758

wind speed, measuring **6**:450–*451*

wind tunnels **1**:*18*, 19; **4**:253

wood and wood carving **5**:331; **10:796–798**

building with wood **2**:108–109

Woolf, Arthur **9**:687

Woolworth Building **9**:646

Volume numbers are in **boldface type** followed by colons. Page numbers in **boldface type** refer to main articles and their illustrations; page numbers in *italic type* refer to picture captions.

wrecking balls **3**:197
Wright, Frank Lloyd **2**:111

X rays, telescopes **10**:730
xylophones **7**:489

Yards (unit of measurement) **6**:425

Zuider Zee **2**:143

INFORMATION TECHNOLOGIES

Ada, Countess of Lovelace **3**:174
aerials *see* antennae
Altair 8800 (computer) **3**:174
ALU (arithmetic-logic unit) **3**:172
amplifiers **1**:35; **5**:370
analog electronics **3**:232, 233
analog technology **3**:206
analog to digital conversion **3**:206
animation **1:39–41**
antennae **1:42–43**; **8**:584
  television **10**:732, *733*
  see also wireless communication
applets **9**:653
arithmetic-logic unit (ALU) **3**:172
artificial intelligence **1:52–54**
ASCII code **3**:172
ATMs (automated teller machines) **1**:*69*
automated teller machines (ATMs) **1**:*69*
autopsies **4**:296

Babbage, Charles **3**:174
Baird, John Logie **10**:*735*
banking **1:68–69**
  security **8**:629–630
bar codes **5**:*367*; **8**:599
Bardeen, John **3**:230, 232
base transceiver stations (BTSs) **10**:*726, 727*
BASIC (computer language) **3**:174; **9**:652
Battleship Potemkin (film) **6**:475
Baudot, Emile **10**:724
Berliner, Emile **9**:658
Berners-Lee, Tim **5**:374
binary code **3**:170, 207; **5**:*367*; **9**:68
  compact discs (CDs) **3**:168–169; **5**:390–391; **9**:689
  computer graphics **3**:176–177
  fax machines **4**:260
  fiber optics **4**:267
Birth of a Nation (film) **6**:475
bitmap (BMP) files **3**:177
Brattain, Walter **3**:230
BTSs (base transceiver stations) **10**:*726, 727*
bytes **9**:688

CAD *see* computer-aided design
cameras **7**:536–539
  digital **3**:*207*; **7**:*537*
  movie **6**:473–474, 476–*477*, 478
  security cameras **8**:*628*
  television **10**:734
Cameron, James **6**:*473*
capacitors, in electronic circuits **3**:231, *233*
cartoons **1**:39
  see also moviemaking
cassettes, tape **9**:659–660
cathode ray tubes **3**:*234*, 235; **10**:*733*, 735

CCTV (closed-circuit television) **8**:*627*, 628; **9**:717
CD *see* compact discs
CD-ROMs **3**:168, 169; **7**:484, 485
CD-Rs (CD-rewriteable discs) **3**:169, 174; **9**:689
  see also digital versatile discs; minidiscs
cellular phones (cell phones) *see* telephony and telegraphy
central processing unit (CPU) **3**:170–172
charge-coupled devices (CCDs) **7**:537; **8**:633; **10**:729, 766
chemotherapy **6**:440
chess, computers playing **1**:*52*, 54
chips *see* integrated circuits
CIM (computer-integrated manufacture) **3**:202
ciphers **2**:156
circuit boards **3**:231
circuit switching **3**:166
closed-circuit television (CCTV) **8**:*627*, 628; **9**:717
codes and ciphers **2:156**
  radio encryption **9**:716
  see also binary code; information theory; Morse code
coins **1**:68
color, and computer graphics **3**:176–177
communication networks **3:166–167**
  and satellites **3**:*167*; **8**:622–623, *624*, 625
  see also telephony and telegraphy

compact discs (CDs) **3:168–169**; **5**:390–391; **8**:633; **9**:660, 689
computer-aided design (CAD) **3**:*203*
  for aircraft **1**:26
  for clothing **2**:150, 151
  for machine tools **6**:417
computer graphics **3:176–177**
  see also animation; moviemaking
computer-integrated manufacture (CIM) **3**:202
computers **3:170–175**
  arithmetic-logic unit (ALU) **3**:172
  central processing unit (CPU) **3**:170–172
  disks and drives **3**:168, 169, 173–174; **9**:688–689
  graphical user interface (GUI) **3**:177; **9**:653
  keyboard **3**:172
  languages **9**:652
  laptop **10**:733–734
  memory **3**:172–173
  monitors **6**:420; **10**:733
  nanocomputers **7**:491
  networks **3**:167; **9**:717–718
  operating system **3**:170

Battery cells use a chemical reaction to generate electricity.

computers (*cont*)
  palmtop *see* personal
    digital assistants
  personal (PCs)
    3:174–175, *202*;
    7:484–485
  processing speed (clock
    speed) **3**:172
  quantum **8**:633
  run using lasers **5**:391
  security **8**:630
  software *see* software and
    programming
  viruses **8**:630
  voice recognition **10**:769
  see also artificial
    intelligence; Internet;
Cooke, William **10**:724
CPU (central processing
  unit) **3**:170–172
credit cards, holograms
  5:347
Crookes, William **8**:583
cryptograms **2**:156

*D*eep Blue (computer) **1**:54
De Forest, Lee **3**:230;
  6:476; **9**:716; **10**:736,
  794
desktop publishing (DTP)
  8:571, 573
digital audio tapes (DATs)
  9:660
digital technology
  3:206–207; **9**:717
  electronics **3**:232–233
  radio **8**:584; **10**:795
  sound recording **9**:660
  telephone signals
    3:166–167;
    10:725–726
  television **3**:207; **10**:736
  video **10**:767–768
digital versatile discs
  (DVDs) **3**:168, 169,
  174; **8**:633; **9**:689;
  10:766, 768
  and multimedia **7**:*484*,
  485

diodes **3**:231, *233*, 234, *235*;
  8:633; **10**:735
  light-emitting (LEDs)
    3:231; **4**:267
Disney, Walt **1**:39
Dolby system **9**:660, 661
domain names **5**:372
doping **8**:632–633
drivers, printer **8**:574
DSL (Digital Subscriber
  Line) **5**:374
Dummer, Geoffrey **5**:370
duplexers **8**:578
DVDs *see* digital versatile
  discs

*E*astman, George **6**:473
Edison, Thomas Alva
  3:230; **6**:411, 474;
  9:658; **10**:724, 735
Eisenstein, Sergei **6**:475
electromagnetic (EM)
  waves,
    1:42, 43
electronic news gathering
  (ENG) **1**:43
electronics **3**:**230–233**
  see also amplifiers;
    computers; integrated
    circuits;
    semiconductors
e-mail **3**:175; **5**:374
encyclopedias, CD-ROM
  7:484, 485
ENIAC **3**:174
Enigma machines **2**:*156*
entomology, forensic **4**:297
expert systems **1**:53
Explorer 1 (satellite) **9**:674
extranets **5**:373

*F*acsimile transmission
  4:**259–260**

Faraday, Michael **10**:793
fax machines *see* facsimile
  transmission
Fellowship of the Ring, The
  (film) **1**:39
fiber optics **3**:*167*;
  4:**266–267**; **5**:326,
  391; **6**:406
  endoscopes **3**:238
  for telephone networks
    9:716; **10**:726
film, photographic
  7:537–538, 539–541
fingerprinting **4**:*296–297*
  genetic **4**:297, 315
"firewalls" (computing)
  8:630
flags **6**:424
Fleischer, Max **1**:39
Fleming, John Ambrose
  10:794
floppy disks **3**:173; **9**:689
fly-by-wire technology **1**:29
focal length **7**:536
forensic science **4**:**296–298**
FORTRAN **9**:652

*G*ance, Abel **6**:475–476
GIF format **3**:177
gigabytes **9**:688
Gladiator (film) **1**:41; **6**:478
Global Maritime Distress
  and Safety System
  (GMDSS) **6**:424
Global Positioning System
  (GPS) **1**:57;
    5:**328–329**; **7**:495;
    8:625; **10**:752
  fishing and **4**:279
  for surveys **9**:709
GMDSS (Global Maritime
  Distress and Safety
  System) **6**:424

Google (search engine) **5**:*374*
GPS *see* Global Positioning
  System
graphical user interfaces
  (GUIs) **3**:177; **9**:653
Griffith, D. W. **6**:475
Groening, Matt **1**:40, 41
GUIs (graphical user
  interfaces) **3**:177;
  9:653

*H*awking, Stephen **10**:*769*
heat sinks **5**:337
Henry, Joseph **10**:793
Hertz, Heinrich **8**:583;
  10:734, 793–794
holovideo **5**:347
HST (Hubble Space
  Telescope) **8**:625;
  9:*665*; **10**:729
HTML *see* Hypertext
  Mark-up Language
HTTP (HyperText
  Transfer Protocol)
  5:374
Hubble Space Telescope
  (HST) **8**:625; **9**:*665*;
  10:729
Huygens, Christiaan **8**:582;
  10:743, 783
Hypertext Mark-up
  Language (HTML)
  5:374; **7**:485; **9**:653
HyperText Transfer
  Protocol (HTTP)
  5:374

*I*cons, computer **3**:177
image compression **3**:207
imaging, multispectral
  8:624
information theory **5**:367
integrated circuits (silicon
  chips; microchips)
  3:172, *174*, 231, 232;
  5:**369–370**; **8**:633;
  manufacture **3**:232;
    5:369–370
  PLCs **3**:228

Volume numbers are in **boldface type** followed by colons. Page numbers in **boldface type** refer to main articles and their illustrations; page numbers in *italic type* refer to picture captions.

integrated services digital network *see* ISDN

intercom systems **6**:455

Internet **3**:175; **5**:372–374; **7**:485

  MP3 controversy **9**:660

  radio **8**:584

  retailing on **8**:598

  security **8**:630

  television **10**:732

Internet Protocol (IP) numbers **5**:372

Internet Service Providers (ISPs) **5**:372, 374

intranets **5**:373

IP (Internet Protocol) numbers **5**:372

ISDN (integrated services digital network) **3**:167, 207; **5**:373; **10**:726, 727

Java (programming language) **9**:653

Jazz Singer, The (film) **6**:476

JPEG format **3**:177

Kilby, Jack **5**:370

kilobytes **9**:688

kinetoscopes **6**:474

Kurzweil, Raymond **10**:769

Landsat satellites **9**:709

languages, multimedia **7**:485

  see also computer

LANs (local area networks) **3**:167

laser disks **10**:767

lasers, in CD players **3**:168, 169; **5**:390–391

LCDs *see* liquid-crystal displays

lenses, camera **7**:536–537, *540*

LEOs (low Earth orbits) **8**:624

light-emitting diodes (LEDs) **3**:231; **4**:267

liquid-crystal displays (LCDs) **3**:*206*; **10**:733–734

  watches with **10**:745

local area networks (LANs) **3**:167

LOES (Low Orbiting Earth Satellites) **3**:167

logic gates **3**:172; **7**:491

loudspeakers **6**:*455*; **9**:658; **10**:725

Lovelace, Ada, Countess **9**:*652*

low Earth orbits (LEOs) **8**:624

Lumière, Auguste and Louis **6**:474

Magnetrons **8**:578

manga films **1**:40

MANs (metropolitan area networks) **3**:167

mapmaking **8**:624; **9**:*709*

Marconi, Guglielmo **8**:583; **9**:*713*, 716; **10**:734–735, *793*, 794, 795

maritime communication **6**:424

megabytes **9**:688

Méliès, Georges **1**:39; **6**:475

metropolitan area networks (MANs) **3**:167

mice (computer input devices) **3**:*172*

microphones and loudspeakers **3**:227, *228*; **6**:453–455; **9**:657–658, *661*; **10**:725, 753

microprocessors **3**:172; **5**:370; **8**:633

  see also integrated circuits

minidiscs **9**:689

modems **5**:373

money **1**:*68–69*

Morse, Samuel **1**:69; **9**:714, 715; **10**:724

Morse code **8**:583; **9**:*714*, 715; **10**:724

moviemaking **6**:473–478

MP3 format and players **3**:207; **9**:660

MPEGs **10**:768

multimedia **3**:175; **7**:484–485

Murnau, E. W. **6**:475

Nanocomputers **7**:491

natural language processing **1**:54

navigation **7**:492–495

  and the Global Positioning System (GPS) **5**:328–329; **7**:495

nickelodeons **6**:474

Nipkow, Paul **10**:735, 736

Nipkow disks **10**:735, *736*

noise **3**:233

Noyce, Robert **5**:370

Pagers **10**:726

palmtops *see* personal digital assistants

Park, Nick **1**:40

PDAs *see* personal digital assistants

personal digital assistants (PDAs; palmtops) **3**:175; **7**:526; **9**:*689*

phonographs **9**:657, 658–659

photocells (photoelectric cells) **3**:233; **4**:259–260

photoconductive cells **4**:260

photocopiers **7**:535

photodiodes **4**:267

photoelectric cells *see* photocells

photoemissive cells **4**:*259*, 260

photography **7**:536–541

  aerial **1**:50; **7**:541

  digital **3**:207; **7**:*537*

photovoltaic cells **4**:260; **9**:655

pixels

  CCD **10**:766

  computer graphics **3**:176–177

  facsimile machines **4**:260

PLCs (programmable logic chips) **3**:228

Poulsen, Valdemar **10**:794

printers, desktop **8**:*574*

programmable logic chips (PLCs) **3**:228

programming, computer *see* software and programming

projectors, movie **6**:478

publishing, desktop (DTP) **8**:571, 573

Quadraphonic sound **9**:661

Aircraft are steered using control surfaces—movable flaps on the wings and tail.

Radar **8**:578–579
and electronic
countermeasures
3:229
fishing and **4**:279
radio **1**:*43*; **8**:582–584;
9:716–717;
10:*793–795*
amplifiers **1**:35
cellular and satellite
phones using **3**:167;
8:582; **10**:*726*
clockwork **5**:*375*
digital **8**:584; **10**:795
frequency bands **1**:43;
8:582; **10**:794
GPS **5**:329
Internet **8**:584
waves **8**:582; **10**:793, 794
see also loudspeaker;
microphone; radar;
television; wireless
communication
records (vinyl discs) **9**:*658,
659*
repeaters **4**:267
Reynaud, Emile **6**:473
Roget, Peter **6**:473
routers **5**:372

Satellites **8**:622–625;
9:674–675
astronomical **8**:624
communications **3**:*167*;
8:622–623, *624*, 625;
10:727
control systems
8:622–623
Global Positioning
System **5**:*328*–329;
7:495; **8**:625
laser-powered **5**:391
launch vehicles
5:*395*–397; **8**:622
military **8**:624–625;
9:692–693
orbits **5**:395; **8**:622, *624*
power systems **8**:623–624
remote-sensing **8**:624

rocket motors **8**:615
weather **6**:451; **8**:*622*, 624
scanners, computer **3**:206
search engines **5**:*374*
semaphore **6**:424; **8**:592
semiconductors **3**:231–232;
5:369–370; **8**:583,
632–633
in solar cells **9**:656
servers, computer **9**:*688*
Shannon, Claude Elwood
5:367
Shockley, William **3**:230
silicon chips *see* integrated
circuits
Simpsons, The (cartoon
show) **1**:*40*, 41
software and programming
3:170; **9**:**651–653**
and computer viruses
8:630
sound recording **9**:**657–661**
for movies **6**:475
speech, recognition and
synthesis **10**:769
Sputnik satellites **9**:674–675
Star Wars (film) **1**:*40*, 41;
6:478
Steadicams **6**:478
storage media **9**:**688–689**
Stuart Little (film) **1**:*41*

Tape
digital audio (DAT) **9**:660
magnetic **9**:659–660
tape recorders **9**:688
TCP/IP **5**:373
Technicolor **6**:477
telecommunications
9:**714–718**
computer networks **3**:167;
9:717–718
see also antennae; radio;

telephony and
telegraphy; television
telephony and telegraphy
8:583; **9**:*714–716*;
10:**724–727**
cellular phones **1**:42;
3:167, 206–207;
8:582; **9**:*716*–717;
10:*726*–727, 795
Internet **5**:*373*
optical fibers **4**:267;
9:716; **10**:726
satellite phones **3**:167;
10:727, *795*
telegraphy for railroad
safety **8**:592
telegraphy to "wire" money
1:69
telephone exchanges
10:725
telephone networks
3:166–167
videophones **1**:43; **9**:717,
718; **10**:727
telescopes **10**:**728–730**
television **9**:717;
10:**731–736**
amplifiers **1**:35
cameras **10**:734
cathode ray tubes **3**:*234,
235*; **10**:733, 735
closed-circuit (CCTV)
8:*627*, 628; **9**:717
color **10**:731–732, *733*
digital **3**:207; **10**:736
electromagnets **6**:420;
10:733
flat panel **10**:736
plasma **10**:736
remote-control **10**:753
Toy Story (film) **1**:41; **3**:177
transducers **6**:453; **10**:725,
753

transistors **3**:230, 231–232,
233; **8**:633; **10**:795
and nanotechnology
7:490, 491
transmitters **1**:*42–43*;
10:732, *733*
triodes **3**:230, 234–235;
10:736
Turing, Alan **1**:53; **3**:170
Turing Test **1**:53, 54

Uniform Resource
Locators (URLs)
5:374
URLs (Uniform Resource
Locators) **5**:374

Vacuum tubes **3**:234, 235
in computers **3**:174
VCRs (video cassette
recorders) **9**:688,
10:766–767
video cassette recorders
(VCRs) **9**:688;
10:766–767
videography **10**:**766–768**
holovideo **5**:347
streaming video **10**:732,
767
surveillance systems **8**:628
videophones **1**:43; **9**:717,
718; **10**:727
virtual reality markup
language (VRML)
7:485
viruses, computer **8**:630
voice recognition **10**:**769**
VRML *see* virtual reality
markup language

WANs (wide area
networks) **3**:167
watermarks (banknotes)
1:69
Watson-Watt, Robert **8**:578
Wheatstone, Charles
10:724
wide area networks (WANs)
3:167; **5**:372

Volume numbers are in **boldface type** followed by colons. Page numbers in **boldface type** refer to main articles and their illustrations; page numbers in *italic type* refer to picture captions.

wireless communication **10:793–795**
wirephotos **4**:260
word processors **9**:653
workstations **3**:177
World Wide Web (WWW) **3**:175; **5**:372, 374; **7**:485
WWW *see* World Wide Web

Xerography **7**:535

Zip disks **3**:173; **9**:689

INDUSTRIAL AND MILITARY TECHNOLOGIES

A-4 rockets **8**:613
Abbe, Ernst **5**:326
accelerometers **6**:452
acetate rayon **4**:270
acid rain **2**:154; **7**:*549, 550*; **8**:567
acids **2**:140–141
actuators **6**:452
adzes **5**:331
aircraft
  detection using radar **8**:*578, 579*
  electronic countermeasures **3**:*229*
  missiles **6**:467
  pilotless **1**:27; **8**:*606–607*
  stealth **1**:*26*, 28; **3**:229; **4**:287; **8**:578
  V/STOL **1**:25
aircraft carriers **1**:24–25; **6**:423
airships **1**:66, 67
alarms, intruder **8**:628

algal blooms **7**:551
alkalis **2**:141
alkylation **7**:513–514
alloys **1**:**34**
aluminum **6**:444, 446
  abundance **7**:517
  in aircraft construction **1**:28
  production **3**:225
  recycling **10**:773
amalgams **6**:447
ammonia **2**:141
  production **2**:125, 140
amphibious vehicles **7**:*502*, 503
anthracite **2**:153; **4**:304
anthrax **2**:133
appliances, household *see* household appliances
aqualungs **3**:193
aquifers **7**:551
Archimedes wave swings (AWSs) **10**:785
argon **4**:308
assembly lines **1**:*58*
atomic energy *see* nuclear energy
Attack Laser program **5**:391
augers **3**:181
automobiles, manufacture **1**:56, *58*
autonomous underwater vehicles (AUVs) **3**:195
AUVs (autonomous underwater vehicles) **3**:195
AWACS aircraft **4**:*283*
AWSs (Archimedes wave swings) **10**:785

Bacteria, and pollution **2**:90; **7**:551
Bakelite **7**:542
Ballistic Missile Early Warning System (BMEWS) **9**:692
bar codes **5**:*367*; **8**:599
barometers **6**:450
Bauhaus **3**:201–202

Baylis, Trevor **5**:*375*
Beams, Jesse **2**:129
Becquerel, Antoine-César **9**:655
beer **2**:88, 89, 90, 98–*99*
Behrens, Peter **3**:200–201
benzene **2**:155
Bessemer, Henry **5**:379, 380; **9**:712–713
binoculars **6**:405–406
biological weapons *see* chemical and germ warfare
bioreactors **2**:*88*, 89
biotechnology **2**:**88–90**
  see also brewing industry
black powder **4**:272; **8**:610
blast furnaces **2**:**91–92**; **5**:379, *381–382*
bleaches **2**:147
bombs and shells **2**:**94–95**
  "smart" bombs **6**:468
  see also missiles; nuclear weapons; torpedoes
boreholes **6**:461
boring mills **6**:416–417
brake lights **3**:201
brand identity **3**:201
brewing industry **2**:**98–99**
bridges, bridging tanks **10**:750
bronze **1**:34; **5**:330
bubble chambers **8**:*581*
buckminsterfullerene **2**:141
bullets **4**:273
  forensic science and **4**:297
butadiene **8**:617

Cableways **2**:158
CAD *see* computer-aided design
calendering machines **10**:740
calorimeters **4**:304
cans
  drink **3**:202
  tin **3**:225
carbon dioxide, and global warming **4**:245, *246–247*, 305; **8**:568
carbon steel **6**:416
Carnegie, Andrew **5**:383
Carothers, Wallace **4**:270, 271, 279
cartridges, firearm **4**:272–273
case hardening **6**:449
cash registers **8**:598–599
casting **2**:**122–123**; **6**:*446*, 448
Castner-Kellner process **3**:225
catalysts **2**:**124–125**, 135; **6**:446
  used in oil refining **7**:513–514
  see also enzymes
cavalry **1**:38
Caxton, William **8**:570
celluloid **7**:545
cellulose **2**:139

Radiant heating systems deliver heat via hot water flowing in pipes.

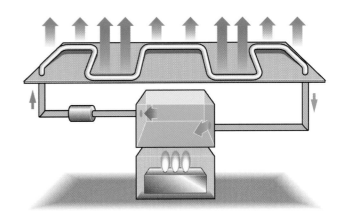

cellulose (*cont*)
  fibers made from **4**:269, 270
cellulose acetate **7**:545
cellulose nitrate **7**:545
centrifugal force **2**:128
centrifuges **2**:128–129
ceramics **2**:130–131
CFCs *see* chlorofluorocarbons
charcoal **2**:91
Chardonnet, Louis-Marie-Hilaire Bernigaud, Count of **4**:270
chemical engineering **2**:134–136; **4**:253
  see also chemical industry
chemical and germ warfare **2**:133
chemical industry **2**:137–141
  see also chemical engineering
chemicals
  inorganic **2**:139–141
  organic **2**:137–139
chisels **5**:331; **10**:798
chlorine, isotopes **2**:129
chlorofluorocarbons (CFCs) **4**:308; **7**:550; **8**:596
  and nanomachines **7**:491
CIM (computer-integrated manufacture) **3**:202
Civil War **4**:*272*, 274
  balloons **1**:66
  iron ships **8**:636
clay **7**:556, 557–558
cleaning agents **2**:146–147
clothing industry **2**:150–152
  see also fibers and yarns; textiles
cloud chambers **8**:581
coal **2**:153–155; **4**:245, 304
  mining **2**:*153*; **6**:*464*, 465
  pollution **4**:246
coal gas (town gas) **4**:304, 306

use in power stations **2**:155
coal tar **2**:138, 155
cochineal **3**:210
Cockerell's rafts **10**:785
coconuts, fibers from **4**:*270*
coke **2**:154, 155; **4**:304; **7**:517
  in iron production **5**:380
Colt .45 (revolver) **4**:*273*
composites, in aircraft construction **1**:28
composting **10**:*774*
computer-aided design (CAD) **3**:*203*
  for clothing **2**:150, 151
  for machine tools **6**:417
computer-integrated manufacture (CIM) **3**:202
Congreve, William **6**:466
conveyors **3**:**181**; **6**:429
copper **6**:446
  ores **7**:516, 517
Cort, Henry **5**:380
cotton **4**:*268*, 269–270; **9**:713; **10**:738
cotton gins **9**:713
Courtelle **4**:271
cracking **2**:125; **7**:510–511, *512*, 513
crude oil *see* oil and natural gas
cyclohexane **2**:*136*

Dacron **4**:271; **9**:678
Dalton, John **2**:139, 140
Darby, Abraham **5**:379–380; **9**:712
deep-sea technology **3**:**192–195**
depth charges **10**:747
derricks **3**:183

design, industrial **3**:**200–203**
detergents **2**:146–*147*
Dickinson, John **7**:523
diffraction **6**:406
dikes **10**:781
dishwashers **10**:*771*
distillation
  fractional **7**:512
  of salt water **10**:779
  vacuum **7**:512
diving, underwater **3**:*192–193*
diving bells **3**:193
draglines **6**:463
drawing, metals **6**:448–449
drills **5**:331
  electric **5**:*331*
drone aircraft **1**:27; **8**:607
dry cleaning **2**:147
Dunlop, John Boyd **8**:616; **10**:746
dyes and dying **2**:138; **3**:165, **210–211**
  mixing **3**:*165*

Earthenware **7**:557
elastomers **8**:616
electricity
  for lighting **6**:410–*411*
  transmission **2**:114; **3**:**215–218**; **8**:566–567
electrochemical machining **6**:417
electrolysis **2**:139–140; **3**:**224–225**
electrolytes **3**:224
electromagnets **7**:516
electron beam machining **6**:417
electronic countermeasures **3**:**229**

electroplating **3**:*225*; **6**:449
ELSBMs (exposed location single buoy moorings) **7**:513
enantiomers **2**:*139*
energy resources **4**:**244–247**
  see also geothermal energy; hydroelectricity; nuclear energy; solar power; wave power; wind power
engineering, military **4**:253
enzymes **2**:90
  brewing and **2**:90, 98
  in detergents **2**:147
  restriction **4**:314
ergonomics **3**:200
etching, glass **1**:13
ethylene **7**:511
Exocet missiles **6**:467
exposed location single buoy moorings (ELSBMs) **7**:513
extinguishers, fire **4**:277
extrusion **6**:*445*, 448; **7**:546
Exxon Valdez (ship) **7**:515
eyeglasses **6**:407, 459

F-117 Nighthawk (stealth aircraft) **1**:*26*; **3**:229; **4**:287
felts **10**:739, 740
fermentation, brewing and **2**:98–99
fermenters **2**:135–136
fibers and yarns **4**:**268–271**; **10**:738
  dyeing **3**:*211*
  see also clothing industry; textiles
files (tools) **5**:331
firearms **4**:**272–274**
  forensic science and **4**:297
firefighting **4**:**275–277**
flashovers **4**:277
flash point **4**:275
flax **4**:269
flintlocks **4**:272

Volume numbers are in **boldface type** followed by colons. Page numbers in **boldface type** refer to main articles and their illustrations; page numbers in *italic type* refer to picture captions.

Flixborough disaster **2**:*136*
flotation, froth **7**:517
flying boats **8**:626
food processors **5**:*352*, 353
footwear
  manufacture **4**:**295**
  sports shoes **9**:*680*
  see also leather
Ford, Henry **1**:55, 56, *58*;
  10:789
Ford, Model T **1**:56;
  10:789
forging **6**:447–448
Fortress America **9**:*693*
fossil fuels **2**:153; **4**:245,
  246, 303, 305; **9**:655
  and global warming **8**:568
  and pollution **7**:548
  see also coal; oil and
    natural gas; peat
foundries, in the United
  States **2**:123
Fourdrinier, Henry and
  Sealy **7**:523
fourdriniers **7**:523, *524*
frit **5**:325
furnaces **5**:379
  blast **2**:**91–92**; **5**:379,
    381–382
  solar **9**:656

Gabor, Dennis **5**:345
gantries **3**:183
garbage disposal **10**:772
gas, natural *see* oil and
  natural gas
gasoline, production
  7:510–511, 513
Gatling, Richard Jordan
  4:274
Gatling guns **4**:274
Geiger counters **8**:581
geophones **7**:505
geothermal energy
  4:**317–318**; **5**:341
Gesner, Abraham **7**:500
glass and glassmaking
  5:**324–326**; **9**:*711*
  etching **1**:13

for optical fibers **4**:267;
  5:326
  recycling **10**:773
global warming **2**:154;
  4:245, *246–247*, 305;
  7:549; **8**:568
Glushko, Valentin **8**:614
gold **6**:444; **6**:461
Gould, Gordon **5**:390
gravimeters **6**:461
gravimetric exploration
  7:505–506
gravure **8**:574
greenhouse effect **7**:549
Gropius, Walter **3**:201
Grumman Flagstaff
  (gunboat) **5**:361
gunboats, hydrofoil **5**:361
guncotton (nitrocellulose)
  4:270
gunpowder **8**:610
  firearms **4**:272, 273
  forensic science and **4**:297
guns *see* firearms
Gutenberg, Johannes **8**:570,
  571

Haber (Haber-Bosch)
  process **2**:125, 140;
  4:265
hair driers **5**:353
Hall, Robert **5**:390
Hall-Héroult process **3**:225
hand tools **5**:**330–331**
Harpoon missiles **6**:467
Harrier jump jets **1**:25
Hawk missiles **6**:467–468
hazardous waste **5**:**334**
heat exchangers **1**:23;
  5:**337**, 341
heat pumps **5**:341
HEAT shells **2**:95
heliostats **9**:656
helium, uses **4**:308
hematite **2**:91; **5**:378
Hercules aircraft **1**:*28*
Hiroshima **7**:*500*
Hoe, Richard March **8**:570
holography **5**:**345–347**, 391

Hoover, William **10**:760
hot dry rock technology
  4:318
household appliances
  5:**352–353**
  electric razors **5**:353
  electric toothbrushes
    5:353
  food processors **5**:*352*,
    353
  hair driers **5**:353
  irons **5**:352–353
  sewing machines **2**:151,
    152; **5**:353
  vacuum cleaners **5**:353;
    10:**760**
  washing machines and
    dishwashers
    10:**770–771**
  see also stoves and ovens
hovercraft, military **5**:354
Howe, Elias **5**:353
hydrants, fire **4**:276
hydrocarbons **2**:138
  from crude oil **7**:511,
    512–513
hydrodesulfurization **7**:513
hydroelectricity **2**:*145*;
  3:216; **4**:247;
  5:**358–359**; **10**:776,
  781
  turbines **5**:358, *359*;
    8:*566*; **10**:*758–759*
hydrofoils, military **5**:361
  see also hovercraft
hydrogenation **2**:125

ICBMs (intercontinental
  ballistic missiles)
  8:613–614, 615
  see also strategic defense
    systems
incinerators **10**:773
inclinometers **6**:420
Industrial Revolution **2**:91;
  4:304; **5**:379–380;
  6:464; **7**:548;
  9:712–713
  water power **10**:776
inks **3**:165; **4**:298
  printing **8**:571
integrated circuits (silicon
  chips; microchips),
  manufacture **3**:232;
  5:369–*370*
inventions **5**:**375–377**;
  9:713
irons **5**:352–353
iron and steel **5**:330,
  378–383; **6**:446
  bridges **2**:102–103;
    5:*383*
  building with **2**:110–111;
    5:*378*; **9**:646, 647
  cast iron **5**:379
  production **2**:*91*–92;
    4:308; **5**:378–383;
    6:*445, 449*; **9**:*713*

The important parts of a modern automobile vary little between one design and another.

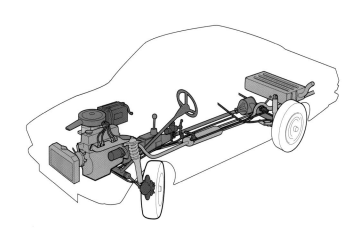

iron and steel (*cont*)
  steel **2**:94; **5**:*379–383*;
    6:*445*, 448, 449
  wrought iron **5**:378
isomerization **7**:514
isotopes, separation **2**:129

Jamming signals **3**:229
jeeps, U.S. Army **7**:502

Kelly, William **5**:379
kerogen **7**:504
kerosene **6**:410; **7**:510
Kevlar **4**:268, *269, 271*
knitting **10**:739
Koenig, Friedrich **8**:570
Korolyov, Sergey **8**:614
krypton **4**:308

Landfills **5**:334; **7**:549;
  10:772
Lanston, Tolbert **8**:570
lasers **5**:**388–391**; **6**:411
  cutting **2**:151; **5**:*389*, 390;
    6:411
  fiber optics **9**:716
  space **9**:693
  to record race winners
    9:681
  used in holography **5**:*345,*
    346–347, 391
  used in surveying
    9:708–709; **10**:757
  weapon-guiding **2**:94, 95;
    5:391
lasing medium **5**:389
lathes **6**:416
Laval, Carl de **2**:128
Lavoisier, Antoine **2**:139,
  140
lead **6**:446
leather **5**:398
leatherette **5**:398
lenses **6**:405–406, *407*
  camera **7**:536–537, *540*
  in microscopes **6**:456
letterpress **8**:571–572
light and optics **6**:**404–407**

and color **3**:164
  fiber optics **3**:*167*;
    4:**266–267**; **5**:326,
    391; **6**:406
light particles **5**:389; **6**:404
light waves **5**:346, 389;
  6:404
  monochromatic light
    5:389
  speed of light **6**:406–407
  telescopes **10**:728, *730*
  ultraviolet light **3**:*164*;
    6:*411*
lights, gas and electric
  9:712
lignite (brown coal) **2**:153,
  154; **4**:304
Linotype **8**:570
liquefied natural gas (LNG)
  4:307
lithography **8**:*572–573*
LNG (liquefied natural gas)
  4:307
locks and safes **6**:**414–415**;
  8:628
Loewy, Raymond **3**:201
looms **10**:*738*, 739, *740*
lost wax process **2**:123
Lowell, Francis Cabot
  10:738
Lucite **7**:544

Machine guns **4**:*274*
machine tools **6**:**416–417**
Macintosh, Charles **8**:616
magazines, gun **4**:274
magnetite **2**:91; **5**:378
magnetometric exploration
  4:306
Maiman, Theodore **5**:390
markets **8**:597–598
marquetry **10**:797, *798*

Martin, Pierre-Emile **5**:381
matchlocks **4**:272
mauveine **2**:138; **3**:210
Maxim, Hiram **4**:274
melamines **7**:543
Mergenthaler, Ottmar
  8:570
metals **6**:**444–449**
  alloys **1**:34
  casting **2**:*122–123*
  corrosion **3**:182
  fatigue **6**:444
  joining **4**:263
  refining **7**:517
  transition **2**:124; **6**:446
  see also iron and steel; ore
    extraction
methane **2**:138, *139*
micromachines **2**:90; **6**:452
  see also nanotechnology
micrometers **5**:*330*, 331
microprinting **1**:69
mines (explosive) **6**:420;
  9:696
mining **6**:**460–465**
  coal **2**:*153*; **6**:*464*, 465
  deep (underground mines)
    2:153; **6**:*462*, 465
  robotic explorers used in
    8:609
  strip (surface mining)
    2:153; **6**:*462*, 465
Mir I and *II* (submersibles)
  3:195
mirrors **6**:*406*
MIRVs **6**:469
missiles **6**:428, **466–469**;
  8:613–614
  Ballistic Missile Early
    Warning System
    (BMEWS) **9**:692
  detected by radar **9**:693

multiple reentry vehicle
  (MRV) missiles **6**:469
National Missile Defense
  (NMD) program
  2:139
see also torpedoes
modular manufacturing
  2:152
molding
  injection-molding **4**:295;
    7:*546*
  plastics **7**:*545*, 546
monomers **2**:138
Monotype **8**:570
moorings, tanker **7**:513
mortars **10**:747
multiple reentry vehicle
  (MRV) missiles **6**:469
Mushet, Robert **5**:380
mustard gas **2**:133

Nanotechnology
  7:**490–491**
  see also micromachines
naphthenes **7**:511
National Missile Defense
  (NMD) program
  2:139
natural gas *see* oil and
  natural gas
Nautilus, USS (submarine)
  6:423; **9**:695
neon **4**:308
neoprene **4**:268, 270; **8**:617
nerve gases **2**:133
newspapers, printing **8**:573
nitric acid **2**:141
nitrocellulose (guncotton)
  4:270
nitrogen
  liquid **4**:308
  uses **4**:307–308
nitroglycerin **4**:273
noble gases **4**:308
nuclear energy **4**:*244*, 247;
  7:**496–499**
nuclear-powered engines
  6:422–423

Volume numbers are in **boldface type** followed by colons. Page numbers in **boldface type** refer to main articles and their illustrations; page numbers in *italic type* refer to picture captions.

nuclear submarines **6**:*421*, 423; **7**:499; **9**:696,

nuclear weapons **7**:**500–501**
  atomic bombs **7**:498, 500–501
  thermonuclear (hydrogen bombs) **7**:499, 501

nylon **4**:270, 271
  for fishing nets **4**:279

Oberth, Hermann **8**:613

oceans
  thermal energy from **10**:777
  wave power **10**:784–785

oil and natural gas **4**:245, 304; **7**:**504–509**
  limited supplies **4**:246
  natural gas **4**:*306–307*
  oil refining **4**:308; **7**:**510–515**

oil shale **7**:509

oil spills **7**:515, 550, 551

oil wells **7**:506–507

open-hearth process **5**:381, *382*

optics *see* light and optics

ore extraction **7**:**516–517**

Orlon **4**:271

oscillating water columns (OWCs) **10**:785

ovens *see* stoves and ovens

oxides **7**:516

oxygen, uses **4**:308

Panthenol **2**:147

paper and papermaking **7**:**522–524**
  recycling **7**:524; **10**:773

parabolic trough solar collectors **9**:656

particle accelerators **6**:420

particleboard **10**:797

Patriot missiles **6**:468

PCBs (polychlorinated biphenyls) **7**:550

peat **2**:153; **4**:245, *304*

Perkin, William **2**:138; **3**:210

PET (polyester terephthalate) **7**:545

petroleum (crude oil) *see* oil and natural gas

pharmaceuticals, industry **7**:533

phenylalanine **2**:*139*

photons **5**:389; **6**:404

pigments **3**:165

pipelines
  bulk materials **10**:762
  oil **7**:514, 515
  water **10**:781

planes **5**:*330*, 331; **10**:*797*, 798

planing machines **6**:417

plastics **2**:138; **7**:**542–546**
  aircraft construction **1**:28
  casting **2**:123
  recycling **7**:546; **10**:773

platinum **6**:446

Plexiglas **7**:544, 546

plutonium, and atomic bombs **7**:500

plywood **10**:797

point of sale **8**:598

pollution **7**:**548–551**
  air **4**:246; **7**:548–550
  bacteria and **2**:90; **7**:551
  by pesticides **7**:529, 550–551
  oil spills **7**:515, 550, 551
  water **2**:*147*; **7**:550–551

polychlorinated biphenyls (PCBs) **7**:550

polyester **4**:271; **10**:738

polyester terephthalate (PET) **7**:545

polyethylene **2**:86, 125, 138; **7**:511, 542, 543
  manufacture **7**:545

polymers **2**:125, 138; **4**:271; **7**:511, 543
  condensation **7**:545

polymethyl methacrylate (PMMA) **7**:544

polypropylene **7**:511, 542, 543

polystyrene **7**:543

polytetrafluoroethylene (PTFE; Teflon) **7**:544

polyvinyl chloride (PVC) **2**:140; **7**:542, 544; **10**:740

porcelain **7**:557, *558*

ports, naval **7**:*552*, 555

potassium **6**:444–445

potassium hydroxide (caustic potash) **2**:141

pottery **7**:**556–558**
  see also ceramics

power stations **3**:215–216, 222; **8**:**566–568**
  burning fossil fuels **5**:358; **8**:566, *567–568*
  gas **4**:304
  geothermal **4**:*318*
  hydroelectric **5**:359–*359*; **8**:566
  IGCC plants **2**:155
  nuclear **4**:*244*, 247; **7**:*498–499*; **8**:566
  oil-fired **8**:567
  solar **4**:252; **9**:656
  thermal **8**:566, 567–568
  use of coal **2**:155; **8**:567

precipitators, electrostatic **8**:567

printing **7**:522–523; **8**:**569–574**
  bank bills **1**:69
  history **8**:570, 571

propylene **7**:511

proteins **2**:139
  fibers made from **4**:269

Prowler (aircraft) **3**:229

PTFE (polytetrafluoroethylene; Teflon) **7**:544

puddling process **5**:380

PVC *see* polyvinyl chloride

Quarrying **6**:462, 463

Radar **8**:**578–579**
  aircraft invisible to *see* stealth aircraft
  missile-detecting **9**:*693*

radiation (ionizing), detection **8**:**580–581**

rafts, Cockerell's **10**:785

rain, acid *see* acid rain

raising machines **10**:740

Rance barrage **10**:777

rasps **10**:798

rayon **4**:270

razors, electric **5**:353

reactors **2**:134, 135–136

recycling **10**:773
  glass **10**:773
  metals **6**:447; **10**:773
  paper **7**:524; **10**:773
  plastics **7**:546; **10**:773

reduction **5**:378
  see also blast furnaces

refining, metals **7**:517

reflection **6**:*404–405*, *406*
  total internal **4**:266; **6**:406

refraction **6**:405

registers, cash **8**:598–599

remotely operated vehicles (ROVs) **3**:195; **10**:749

retail industry **8**:**597–599**
  store security **8**:628, *629*

revolvers **4**:*273*, 274

rifling **4**:273

rigs, oil **7**:506, 507–*508*
  see also oil refining

Rittenhouse, William **7**:523

Robert, Nicholas-Louis **7**:523

robotics **1**:*54*; **8**:**608–609**; **9**:677

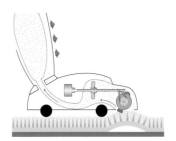

In an upright vacuum cleaner, beater bars shake the carpet to loosen dirt, and brushes sweep surface litter.

robotic inspectors **8**:609; **10**:749

for telesurgery **6**:442

rooms, strong **6**:415

ROVs *see* remotely operated vehicles

rubber **8**:**616–617**; **10**:746

Safeguard system **9**:692

safes *see* locks and safes

Salter's ducks **10**:*784–785*

sandblasting **1**:*12*, 13

sandpaper **10**:798

sarin **2**:133

satellites, military **8**:**624–625**; **9**:692–693

sawmills **4**:300

saws **5**:331; **10**:798

power **6**:417

SBLs (space-based lasers) **9**:693

Schawlow, Arthur **5**:390

Schott, Otto **5**:326

Sea Skua missiles **6**:467

seawater, distillation **10**:779

security equipment **8**:**627–630**

at airports **1**:33; **8**:628–629, *630*

see also locks and safes

Senefelder, Aloys **8**:570, 572

Sentinel system **9**:692

septic tanks **10**:774

sewage, treatment **10**:**773–775**

sewing machines **2**:151, 152; **5**:353

shampoos **2**:147

shells *see* bombs and shells

ships and boats, building **8**:**636–638**

shoes *see* footwear

shops *see* retail industry

shot **4**:273

shot blasting **1**:13

Shrapnel, Henry **2**:95

Sidewinder missiles **6**:467, 468

Siemens, William **5**:380

silencers **4**:274

silk **4**:269

silver **6**:446, 447

ski lifts **2**:158

slopers **2**:150, 151

smelting **6**:447; **7**:517

soaps **2**:*146*

sodium **6**:444–445

production **3**:225

sodium hydroxide (caustic soda) **2**:141

solar cells **8**:633; **9**:655, 656

solar panels **5**:*338*, 341

on satellites **8**:623

solar power **3**:216; **4**:*245*, 246; **9**:**655–656**

for satellites **8**:623

sonar

for fishing **4**:279

for navigation **9**:*695*

space-based lasers (SBLs) **9**:693

Spandex **10**:738

Spangler, James Murray **10**:760

spinnerets **4**:270

spinning **4**:268; **9**:*712*; **10**:738

spokeshaves **10**:797–798

sports technology **9**:**680–681**

sputtering **5**:370

starch **2**:139

"Star Wars" **9**:693

stealth aircraft **1**:*26*, 28; **3**:229; **4**:287; **8**:578

steel *see* iron and steel

stock control **8**:599

stoneware **7**:557

see also ceramics

stoves and ovens **5**:339; **9**:**690–691**

microwave ovens **5**:*353*; **9**:*691*

strategic defense systems **9**:**692–693**

styrene **2**:138

submarines **9**:**695–697**

depth charges and **10**:747

miniature **9**:696

nuclear **6**:*421*, 423; **7**:499; **9**:696, *697*

submersibles **3**:*193*, *195*; **9**:696

sulfides **7**:516

sulfur dioxide, and acid rain **7**:*549*; **8**:567

sulfuric acid **2**:140–141

superalloys **1**:34

supercarriers **1**:25

superconductors **2**:141

surfactants **2**:146, 147

Tags, electronic **8**:628, *629*

tanks **2**:95; **7**:502; **10**:**748**, *749–750*

tannins **5**:398

tar sands **7**:509

technology, history of **9**:**710–713**

Teflon **7**:544

Tencel **4**:270

Terylene **4**:271

textiles **10**:**737–740**

dyeing **3**:*211*

see also clothing industry; fibers and yarns

thermoplastics **1**:16; **7**:542, 546

thermosetting plastics (thermosets) **1**:16; **7**:542–543

tidal energy **10**:777

tills **8**:598

tin **6**:447

titanium, in aircraft construction **1**:28

TNT (trinitrotoluene) **2**:94

tools

hand **5**:**330–331**

invention **5**:375

machine **6**:**416–417**

power tools **10**:798

toothbrushes, electric **5**:353

torpedoes and depth charges **10**:747

Townes, Charles H. **5**:390

town gas *see* coal gas

Trans-Alaska pipeline **7**:515

traps, geological **7**:*505*

Triton (submarine) **9**:695

tumbling mills **1**:13

Turtle (submarine) **9**:695

typesetting **8**:569–571

Typhoon submarines **9**:697

tyrian purple **3**:210

UAVs *see* unpiloted aerial vehicles

U-boats **9**:695

ultracentrifuges **2**:128, 129

ultrasonic machining **6**:417

unpiloted aerial vehicles (UAVs) *see* drone aircraft

uranium

and atomic bombs **7**:500

isotopes **2**:129; **7**:498, 499

V-1 missiles **6**:468

V-2 rockets **6**:*468*; **8**:613, *614*, 615

vacuum cleaners **5**:353; **10**:760

veneer **10**:797

Vietnam War, hovercraft **5**:354

viscose process **4**:270

vitrification **7**:557

von Braun, Wernher **8**:613, 615

V/STOL aircraft **1**:25

vulcanization **8**:617; **10**:746

Volume numbers are in **boldface type** followed by colons. Page numbers in **boldface type** refer to main articles and their illustrations; page numbers in *italic type* refer to picture captions.

Washing machines and dishwashers **5:**352; **10:770–771**
waste treatment **10:772–775**
hazardous waste **5:334**
landfills **5:334**; **7:549**; **10:**772
water power **10:776–777**
see also hydroelectricity
water resources **10:778–781**
waterwheels **10:**776, 777
Watson-Watt, Robert **8:**578
wavelength **3:**164; **5:**389; **6:**404; **10:**783
wave power **10:784–785**
weaving **10:738–739**
wells **10:**780
welting **4:**295
whaling **4:**280
Whitehead, Robert **10:**747
Whitney, Eli **9:**713
windmills **10:**790, 791–792
wind power **3:**216; **4:**247; **10:**759, **790–792**
wood and wood carving **5:**331; **10:796–798**
cellulose from wood **4:**270
paper from wood pulp **7:**524
wood as a fuel **4:**246, 305
wool **4:**268, 269, 271; **10:**738
dyeing **3:**211
World War I
tracked vehicles **10:**748, 750
zeppelins **1:**67
World War II
amphibious trucks **7:**502
attack on Pearl Harbor **1:**24
bombs **2:**94
Liberty ships **8:**635
nuclear weapons **7:**500
radio **8:**583
submarines **9:**695
torpedoes **10:**747

Xenon **4:**308

Yale, Linus, Jr. **6:**414, 415
yarns *see* fibers and yarns

Zeiss, Carl **5:**326
zeolites **2:**125
zeppelins **1:**67
zinc **6:**447

MEDICINE

Agonists **7:532–533**
AIDS **5:**366
allergies **5:**365, 366
alternative therapies **7:**530
Alzheimer's disease **7:**530
amalgams, dental **3:198–199**
ampicillin **1:**44
analgesics **7:**533
anemia **7:**531
anesthetics **6:**441; **9:**704, 705
angiography **6:**434
angioscopes **3:**238
anthrax **2:**133
antibiotics **1:44–45**; **2:**139; **6:**440; **7:**532
antibodies **5:364–365**
and cancer **2:**121
antidepressants **7:**534
antipsychotic drugs **7:**534
antiseptics **1:46–47**; **7:**531; **9:**704
appendectomy **9:**705, 706
arms, artificial **2:**87
arthritis, rheumatoid **5:**366; **7:**530
aspirin **7:**532
autoclaves **1:**47
autoimmunity **5:365–366**
autopsies **9:**703

Bacteria
and antibiotics **1:**44, 45
and antiseptics **1:46–47**
and biotechnology **2:**88, *89, 90*
Banting, Frederick Grant **7:**534
barber-surgeons **9:**703
Bassi, Agostino **1:**44
B-cells **5:**365
bends, the **3:192–193**
Bernard, Claude **7:**532
Best, Charles H. **7:**534
bionics (biomedical engineering) **2:86–87**; **4:**255; **6:**443
biopsies **3:**205; **9:**704
bioreactors **2:**88, 89
biosensors **2:**90; **6:**439
biotechnology **2:88–90**
genetic engineering **1:**36; **2:**89; **4:314–316**; **7:**529
birth control **7:**534
Black Death **10:**765
blood
cells **5:**364
tests **3:**204
transfusions **2:**93
bloodletting **9:**703
blood pressure **3:**204; **6:**439
high **7:**534
bone marrow, transplants **5:**366
borescopes **3:**238
braces, teeth **3:**199
brain, electroencephalo-grams (EEGs) **6:**440

Cancer
causes **2:**120
treatments **2:120–121**; **6:**440
CAT scans *see* computed tomography
cauterization **9:**702
cells
biotechnology and **2:88–89**
organelles **2:**129
chemotherapy **2:**121
chlorhexidine **10:**764
chloroform **6:**441
chromosomes **4:**314
cinchona **7:531–532**
cloning **1:**36; **2:148–149**
sheep **2:**148, 149
cochlear implants **2:**87
computed tomography (computerized axial tomography) **3:**205; **6:**435, 439
computerized axial tomography *see* computed tomography
computers, in medicine **6:**439
cosmeses **2:**87
crowns, dental **3:**199
cryosurgery **6:**442

Archeologists use the pattern of tree rings in wooden finds to figure out when the trees were alive.

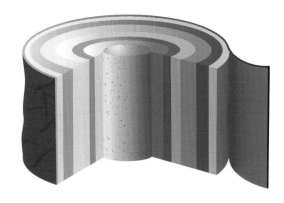

CT *see* computed tomography
curare **7**:532

Deaf people, cochlear implants **2**:87
defibrillators **6**:443
dentistry **3**:198–199
  drills **1**:*13*
dentures **3**:199
diabetes **6**:439; **7**:534
diagnostic equipment **3**:204–205
  see also medical imaging
dialysis **6**:443
digitalis **7**:*532*
Dioscorides **7**:531
disease(s)
  animal **10**:764–765
  the immune system and *see* immunology
  see also medical technology
disinfectants **1**:*46, 47*
DNA **4**:*314*
  analysis **3**:205
  DNA fingerprinting **4**:297, 315
  genetic engineering and **2**:89; **4**:314, *315*, 316
  nanotechnology **7**:491
  recombinant **4**:314, *316*
DNA ligase **4**:314
Dolly (sheep) **2**:*148*, 149
drugs, therapeutic *see* antibiotics; medical technology; pharmacology

Ears, cochlear implants **2**:87
ECGs (electrocardiograms) **6**:440
EEGs (electroencephalograms) **6**:439-*440*
Ehrlich, Paul **1**:44
electrocardiograms (ECGs) **6**:439-*440*
electroencephalograms (EEGs) **6**:440

endoscopes **3**:238; **6**:437, *442*–443; **9**:704
engineering
  biomedical (bionics) **2**:86–87; **4**:255
  genetic **1**:36; **2**:89; **4**:314–316; **7**:529
enzymes **2**:90
  drugs affecting **7**:532
  genetic engineering **4**:314
  restriction **4**:314
Escherichia coli (*E. coli*)
  and food poisoning **4**:294
  and genetic engineering **2**:89, *90*; **4**:314
ether **6**:441
eyeglasses **6**:407, 459
eyes, laser surgery **5**:390–391

Farsightedness **6**:407
fat(s), body **4**:291
fiberscopes **3**:238
filters, air **1**:47
Fleming, Alexander **1**:44, *45*
food poisoning **4**:294

Gamma rays, for sterilization **1**:47
gastroscopes **3**:238
gene therapy **2**:121
genetic engineering **1**:36; **2**:89; **4**:314–316; **7**:529
Gibbon, John H. **5**:336
grenades **2**:95

Harvey, William **9**:704
hay fever **5**:*365*
hearing **1**:14
heart, electrocardiograms (ECGs) **6**:439–440

heart attacks, chaos theory and **2**:132
heart disease **7**:534
heart-lung machines **5**:335–336
heparin **5**:336
hips, artificial **2**:86–87
histamine **5**:366
HIV **5**:366
hormone replacement therapy (HRT) **7**:534
hormones, drugs based on **7**:534
horses
  animal transportation **1**:37–38
  fitness **10**:765
Human Genome Project **4**:316
humans, cloning **2**:149
hyperopia **6**:407
hypnotic drugs **7**:534

ICUs *see* intensive care units
imaging, medical *see* medical imaging
immunology **5**:364–366
influenza **1**:45
injections, drug **7**:530
insulin **6**:439; **7**:534
  biotechnology and **2**:*89*, *90*; **4**:316
intensive care units (ICUs) **5**:371; **6**:443
interferons **2**:121
iodine, antiseptics based on **1**:46
isopropyl alcohol **1**:46

Jenner, Edward **5**:*366*
joints (body), replacement **2**:86–87

Landsteiner, Karl **2**:93
lasers
  surgery using **5**:*390–391*; **9**:*705*
  used in dentistry **3**:199
legs, artificial **2**:87
Lenard, Philipp **6**:436
lice, head **6**:*459*
ligands **7**:532
limbs, artificial **2**:87
linear accelerators **2**:*120*
Lister, Joseph **1**:46; **9**:704
lymphocytes **5**:365

Mad cow disease **6**:412; **10**:765
magnetic resonance imaging (MRI) **3**:*204*; **6**:420, *435*–436, 439
masers **5**:390
Mayo brothers **9**:703
medical imaging **6**:434–437, 439
  dentistry **3**:198
  endoscopy **3**:238; **6**:437
  see also diagnostic equipment; medical technology
medical technology **6**:438–443
  see also heart-lung machines; intensive care unit; medical imaging
mercury, antiseptics based on **1**:46
microbots **8**:609
microorganisms
  sources of antibiotics **1**:44
  see also bacteria
microscopy **6**:438, 439, **456–459**
morphine **7**:532–533
MRI scans **3**:*204*
myopia **6**:407

Neuroma, acoustic **6**:436

Olds, Ransom Eli **1**:55

Volume numbers are in **boldface type** followed by colons. Page numbers in **boldface type** refer to main articles and their illustrations; page numbers in *italic type* refer to picture captions.

operating rooms **9**:*703*, 705–706

opiates **7**:533

Pacemakers, heart **2**:87
painkillers **7**:532–533
Pasteur, Louis **1**:44; **6**:438
pathenogenesis **2**:149
PCR (polymerase chain reaction) **3**:205
penicillin **1**:*44*, 45
Penicillium **1**:*44*, *45*
phagocytes **5**:364
pharmaceuticals **7**:530
pharmacology **7**:**530–534**
  see also antibiotics; medical technology
pharmacopoeias **7**:532
phenol **1**:46
physiology **9**:703–704
plague **10**:765
plasma, blood **2**:93
platelets **2**:93; **5**:364
pollen, allergies to **5**:*365*
polymerase chain reaction (PCR) **3**:205; **4**:297
polymerases **4**:314
positron emission tomography (PET) **6**:437, 439
Prontosil Red **1**:44
prostheses **2**:87
Prozac **7**:534

Quarantine, animal **10**:764–765

Radiation, medical uses **7**:497
radiography, digital **3**:198
radioisotopes **3**:205
radiotherapy **2**:*120*, 121
resistance meters, electrical **1**:50
retina **3**:164; **6**:407
rhinoplasty **9**:706
rods and cones **3**:164
Röntgen, Wilhelm Konrad **6**:434, 436

Salicin **7**:532
Salmonella **4**:294
Salvarsan **1**:44
sheep, cloning **2**:*148*, 149
shortsightedness **6**:407
sick building syndrome **1**:23
smallpox **2**:133; **5**:366
smog **7**:548
sphygmomanometers **3**:204; **6**:439
staples, surgical **9**:706
sterilization, of germs **1**:46–47; **6**:*442*
stethoscopes **6**:438
stitches, surgical **9**:706
streptomycin **1**:44
sulfonamides **1**:45
surgery **6**:441–443; **9**:**702–706**
  cancer **2**:120–121
  cosmetic **9**:706
  cryosurgery **6**:442
  diagnostic **9**:704
  heart-lung machines **5**:335–336
  keyhole **6**:437, 442–443; **9**:704
  laser **5**:*390–391*; **9**:*705*

Tablets, medical **7**:530
tannins **7**:531
T-cells, helper **5**:365
telemedicine **6**:439
telesurgery **6**:442
thermography **10**:742
tomosynthesis **3**:198
tranquilizers **7**:534
transfusions, blood **2**:**93**
transplants, organ **5**:366; **9**:704
trephination **9**:702
twins **2**:148

Ultrasound, scans **3**:205; **6**:436–437, 439
ultraviolet light, for sterilization **1**:47
urine, testing **3**:204–205

Vaccination **5**:*364*, 365, *366*
Valium **7**:534
ventilating machines **5**:*371*
veterinary medicine **10**:**763–765**
vision **3**:164

X rays **3**:198, 205; **6**:*434*, *437*, 439, *443*
  for sterilization **1**:47
  see also computed tomography

Zoonoses **10**:765

TRANSPORTATION

2001 Mars Odyssey (space probe) **9**:669
Aaron Manby (ship) **8**:636
Acela trains **6**:427
Ackerman system **1**:61
aerodynamics **1**:**17–19**
ailerons **4**:286; **5**:327
airbags **1**:59; **6**:*452*
aircraft
  autopilots **7**:*494*
  brakes **2**:97
  construction **1**:26–27, *29*
  control systems **1**:28–29
  crop-spraying **3**:*186*, 187
  delta-winged **4**:287
  design **1**:26–29; **4**:287
  detection using radar **8**:*578*, *579*
  displays on cockpit windows **5**:347
  electronic countermeasures **3**:*229*
  engines **1**:27, 28, **30**; **4**:311
  flight **1**:18, *19*; **4**:**282–287**
  jet **1**:28; **4**:287, 311; **6**:428
  main components **1**:*29*
  micromachines and **6**:452
  paint **7**:*521*
  pilotless **1**:27; **8**:606–607
  seaplanes **8**:**626**
  and sonic booms **1**:18, *19*
  "super jumbo" **1**:27
  tires **8**:617
  see also aerodynamics; airports and airfields; balloons; gliders; helicopters
aircraft carriers **1**:24–25; **6**:423
air-cushion vehicles *see* hovercraft
airliners **1**:27, 28
airports and airfields **1**:**31–33**; **2**:143

Space probes use the gravity of Jupiter to speed them on their way to observe Saturn at close quarters.

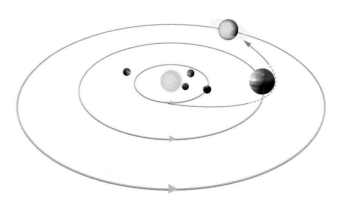

airport surveillance radar (ASR) **8**:579
security **1**:33; **8**:628–629, *630*
airships **1**:66, *67*
air-traffic control **1**:33
alcohol, as a fuel **4**:*305*
all-terrain vehicles (ATVs) **7**:*503*
alternators **4**:251
Alvin (submersible) **3**:195
amphibious vehicles **7**:*502*, 503
Amphicars **7**:503
animal transportation **1:37–38**; **9**:*649*
antilock braking system (ABS) **2**:97
Apollo space program **9**:675–676
aqualungs **3**:193
Ariane rockets **5**:397
astrolabes **7**:493
ATC (automatic train control) systems **8**:593–594
Atlantis (space shuttle) **9**:*670, 674*
ATVs (all-terrain vehicles) **7**:503
autogiros **5**:344
automated people movers (APMs) **8**:607
automatic train control (ATC) systems **8**:593–594
automobiles **1:55–59**
aerodynamics **1**:*18*, 19
brake lights **3**:201
brake systems **1**:59; **2**:96–97; **5**:*357*
computers on **1**:57
cooling **1**:58; **5**:337
design **1**:19, *57*
electric **3**:223
electrical system **1**:59, *71*; **5**:362–367
engine **1**:57–58; **5**:362
exhaust systems **1**:57–58

first **1**:55; **5**:*376*, 377
four-wheel drive **1**:59
fuel **4**:309
fuel intake systems **1**:57
hybrid **3**:223
ignition systems **1**:57; **5**:*362–363*
instrument panel **10**:753
lubrication **1**:58
safety systems **1**:59
steering **1**:59, **60–61**
suspension **1:62–63**
tires **1**:59; **8**:*617*; **10**:*761*, 789
transmission systems **1**:57; **4**:*313*; **5**:*357*; **6**:*429*–430
wheels **1**:59, 60
see also race cars
autonomous underwater vehicles (AUVs) **3**:195
autopilots **7**:*494*
Auto Train **8**:587
AUVs (autonomous underwater vehicles) **3**:195
AWACS aircraft **4**:*283*

Balloons **1:66–67**
barges **2**:119
Barton, Otis **3**:194
bathyspheres **3**:194
Beebe, Charles **3**:194
Bell, Alexander Graham **5**:360; **9**:714–715, 716; **10**:*725*
Bell Model 47 (helicopter) **5**:344
Benz, Karl **1**:55; **5**:377
Bernouilli effect **4**:282
bicycles **1:76–78**
brakes **1**:77–78; **2**:96
streamlined **1**:*17*

tires **10**:746
transmission system and gears **1**:76–77, *78*; **6**:*429*, 430
biofuels **4**:305
Blucher (locomotive) **8**:587
boats *see* ships and boats
bobsledding **9**:649
boilers, steam engine **9**:682, 683
brake systems **2:96–97**
automobile **1**:59; **2**:96–97; **5**:*357*
bicycle **1**:77–78; **2**:96
motorcycle **6**:472
railroad car **8**:585
Branson, Richard **1**:67
Breitling Orbiter 3 (balloon) **1**:67
Buenos Ayrean (ship) **8**:636
buggies, dune **7**:503
bulk carriers **6**:*423*; **7**:554
buoys **6**:409; **7**:553–554
buses **2:113**

Cable cars **2**:158
cableways **2**:158
caissons **2**:118–119
calorific value **4**:304
camels **1**:*37*
canals **2:115–119**
elevators **2**:119; **3**:237
canoes, dugout **8**:634, *635*
Cape Canaveral **5**:392, *393*
carburetors **4**:251
cargo
air **1**:33
ships' **7**:*554–555*
carvel construction **8**:636
Cassini (space probe) **9**:*669*
catalytic converters **1**:57–58; **2**:125

tires **10**:746
catamarans **8**:565
cavitation **5**:361; **9**:644
centralized traffic control (CTC) **8**:594
Challenger (space shuttle) **5**:397; **9**:676
Champ racing **8**:576
chronometers **5**:328; **7**:*493*, 494–495
Cierva, Juan de la **5**:343, 344
Clementine (space probe) **9**:666
clinker boats **8**:636
Cockerell, Christopher **5**:354
cog railroads **2:157–158**
compasses **6**:418; **7**:493–*494*
Comuta (car) **3**:223
Concorde (aircraft) **1**:27
containers **8**:586, *634*
Contour (space probe) **9**:669
Corinth Canal **2**:*117*, 118
Cousteau, Jacques **3**:193
crankshafts **4**:248–249
crawlers **10**:748, 750, 751
cross staffs **7**:493
CTC (centralized traffic control) **8**:594
Cugnot, Nicolas-Joseph **9**:686

Daimler, Gottlieb **1**:55; **5**:*376*, 377
Dawn (space probe) **9**:667
deep-sea technology **3:192–195**
Deep Space 1 (space probe) **9**:668–669
dhows **8**:621
Discovery (space shuttle) **5**:*394*
distributors **5**:363
diving, underwater **3**:*192–195*
diving bells **3**:193, 194
Docklands Light Railway **8**:*607*
dogsledding **9**:649

Volume numbers are in **boldface type** followed by colons. Page numbers in **boldface type** refer to main articles and their illustrations; page numbers in *italic type* refer to picture captions.

donkeys **1**:37, 38

drag, effect on an airplane **4**:*283*

drag racing **8**:577

drone aircraft **1**:27; **8**:607

Dunlop, John Boyd **1**:76; **10**:746

Duryea, Charles and James **1**:55

dynamometers **8**:619

E costar (car) **3**:223

electric road vehicles **3**:**223**

elephants **1**:38

elevators (aircraft control surfaces) **4**:286

elevators (lifts), canal **2**:119; **3**:237

Ely, Eugene **1**:*25*

engines **4**:**248–251**
  aircraft **1**:30
  automobile **1**:57–58; **5**:362
  ceramics used in **2**:131
  diesel **2**:157; **4**:*251*; **5**:362; **6**:422, *423*; **8**:587–588
  external combustion **4**:249, 311
  gasoline **4**:*249*–250, 251
  ignition systems **5**:**362–363**
  in-line **1**:30
  internal combustion **4**:249–251
  ion **8**:615
  jet **1**:30; **6**:*427*, 428
  motorcycle **6**:471–472
  outboard and inboard **8**:564
  radial **1**:30
  reciprocating **9**:683
  rocket **5**:395, 396; **8**:*611*
  rotary **1**:30; **9**:683
  steam *see* steam engines
  Stirling (gas engines) **4**:311
  V-type **1**:30
  see also gas turbines and engines

Environmental Concept Buses (ECBs) **2**:113

equator **7**:492

escalators **4**:**256**; **6**:429

Evans, Oliver **9**:686

expendable launch vehicles (ELVs) **5**:396

extravehicular mobility units (EMUs) **9**:677–678

F -117 Nighthawk (stealth aircraft) **1**:*26*; **3**:229; **4**:287

ferries
  hovercraft **5**:354
  hydrofoil **5**:361
  roll-on, roll-off **7**:554; **8**:*637*

fire trucks **4**:*275*, 276

flatbeds **8**:586

flight **1**:18, *19*; **4**:**282–287**
  helicopter **5**:342
  robotic **8**:**606–607**
  space **9**:**662–664**
  see also aerodynamics; aircraft; balloons; glider

floatplanes **8**:626

fly-by-wire technology **1**:29

flying boats **8**:626

flywheels **9**:683

Ford, Henry **1**:55, 56, *58*; **10**:789

Ford, Model T **1**:56; **10**:789

Formula One cars **8**:576

freeways **8**:605

fuel injection systems **4**:251

fuels and propellants **4**:273, **303–305**

Fulton, Robert **9**:686, 713

G agarin, Yuri **8**:613; **9**:675

Galileo (space probe) **9**:*668*

Garnerin, André-Jacques **7**:525

gas industry **4**:**306–308**

gasoline **2**:155; **4**:304, **309**

gas turbines and engines **4**:**310–311**; **6**:422
  helicopter **5**:344

Géant, Le (balloon) **1**:66

Gemini spacecraft **9**:*679*

Genesis (space probe) **9**:669

Giffard, Henri **1**:30, 67

Giotto (space probe) **9**:669

Glenn, John **9**:675

gliders **5**:327
  see also flight

Goodyear, Charles **8**:617

Great Britain (ship) **8**:636

Great Eastern (ship) **8**:636

GT racing **8**:577

Gurney, Goldsworthy **9**:686–687

gyroscopes **6**:470; **7**:494, 495

H ALO and HAHO techniques **7**:525

Harrier jump jets **1**:*25*

Harrison, John **5**:328; **7**:*493*, 494–495

headlights, ultraviolet **2**:113

helicopters **5**:**342–344**

heptane **4**:309

Hercules aircraft **1**:*28*

highways *see* roads

Hindenburg (airship) **1**:67

horses **1**:*38*
  tack and horseshoes **1**:38

hovercraft **5**:**354–355**

HPVs (human-powered vehicles) **1**:78

hulls **8**:564, 635
  displacement **8**:565
  longship **8**:620–621
  testing **8**:619

human-powered vehicles (HPVs) **1**:78

hybrid vehicles **3**:223

hydrofoils **5**:**360–361**

I cebreakers **9**:650

ignition systems **1**:57; **5**:**362–363**

Indianapolis 500 (Indy 500) **8**:577

International Space Station **4**:*252*; **8**:625; **9**:*672–673*

Interstate Highway System, U.S. **8**:603

isooctane **4**:309

J *ahre Viking* (ship) **7**:515, 552

jeeps, U.S. Army **7**:502

jetfoils **5**:*361*

Jones, Brian **1**:67

junks **8**:621

Jupiter, space probes to **9**:668–669

K aiser, Henry **8**:635

karting **8**:576–577

keels **8**:621

Kennedy Space Center **5**:392, *394*

Kepler (space probe) **9**:667

kerosene **4**:304

A seismograph uses the movement of a weight connected to a pen to draw a seismogram, which shows an earthquake.

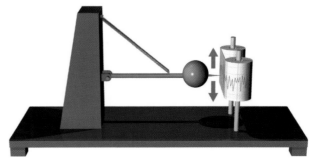

Kittinger, Joseph **1**:67
knocking **4**:251, 309; **5**:363
knots (speed) **7**:495

Lₐ Mountain, John **1**:66
lateens **8**:621
latitude **7**:492, 493
launch sites **5:392–394**
launch vehicles **5:395–397**;
    9:662
Lenormand, Louis-
    Sebastien **7**:525
Liberty ships **8**:635
lift **4**:*282, 283*
lighthouses **6:408–409**
lightships **6**:409
Lindstrand, Per **1**:67
liners **8**:638
liquefied petroleum gas
    (LPG) **4**:304, 307
llamas **1**:37
locks, canal **2**:116–117, *119*
Locomotion (locomotive)
    8:587
longitude **5**:328; **7**:492, *493*,
    494–495
Long March rockets **5**:*395*,
    397
longships **8**:620–621
luges **9**:649
Lunar Orbiter space probes
    9:666
Lunar Prospector (space
    probe) **9**:666
Luna space probes **9**:666
Lunik space probes
    9:665–666

*M*ₐgellan (space probe)
    9:*666*, 667
maglevs (magnetic
    levitation systems)
    6:*418*, 419, 470
Mariner space probes
    9:666, 667, 668
Mars, space probes to
    9:667–668, 669
Mars Global Surveyor (space
    probe) **3**:*167*; **9**:667

marshaling yards **8**:*593*, 594
Marsh, Sylvester **2**:157
Mars Pathfinder (space
    probe) **9**:667–668
Mauretania (ship) **9**:687
Mercury, space probes to
    9:667, 668
meridian, prime **7**:492
methanol **4**:307
micrometeors **9**:*663*
Mir (space station) **8**:625;
    9:*670*, 671, 672
Mir I and *II* (submersibles)
    3:195
monomobiles **6**:470
monorails **6:470**
Montgolfier, Joseph and
    Jacques **1**:66
Moon
    landings **5**:*377*; **9**:675–676
    space probes to **9**:665–666
mopeds **6**:471
motion, third law of **4**:311
motorcycles **6:471–472**
mules **1**:38

*N*ₐvigation **7:492–495**
    and the Global
    Positioning System
    5:328–329; **7**:495
NEAR Shoemaker (space
    probe) **9**:667, 669
NERVA rockets **8**:615
Newcomen, Thomas **6**:427;
    9:685–686
North Star **7**:493

*O*ff-road vehicles
    7:502–503
O'Hare International
    Airport **1**:*31*, 32
oil, automobile engine **1**:58
Olds, Ransom Eli **1**:55

Pₐck animals **1**:37
paddle steamers **6**:422
Panama Canal **2**:116, 118
Pan-American Highway
    8:605
parachutes **7:525**
Parsons, Charles **9**:687
Piccard, Bertrand **1**:67
pickle-fork boats **8**:565
pickups **10**:755
pilots, harbor **7**:552
Pioneer space probes **9**:666,
    668
pitch (torque) **4**:*282*, 285
Pitman arms **1**:60–61
planes, inclined, on canals
    2:117–118
planing **8**:564
Polaris **7**:493
pontoon boats **8**:565
ports **2**:143; **7:552–555**
powerboats **8:564–565**
propellants **4**:305
    firearm **4**:273
propellers, ship **2**:*123*;
    9:644
Proton rockets **5**:397

*Q*ueen Elizabeth II (ship)
    8:638
Quimby, Harriet **4**:287

Rₐce cars **1**:19;
    8:576–577; **10**:746,
    789
racing, motorcycle **6**:472
rack and pinion systems
    1:61
radar **8:578–579**
    aircraft invisible to *see*
        stealth aircraft
railroad cars **8:585–588**
railroad locomotives **8**:587

railroads
    cable-operated **2**:158
    cog **2:157–158**
    construction **8:589–591**
    gauge **8**:585
    operation **8:592–594**
    points **3**:228; **8**:*594*
    signals **8**:*592–593*, 594
    U.S. mileage **8**:589
    see also subway systems;
        trains
Rainbow (ship) **8**:636
Ranger space probes **9**:666
reefers **10**:755
remotely operated vehicles
    (ROVs) **3**:195; **10**:749
Remote Manipulator
    System (RMS) **9**:677
reusable launch vehicles
    (RLVs) **5**:396
roads **8:600–605**
road trains **10**:755
robotic flight **8:606–607**
Rocket (locomotive) **8**:587
rockets **8:610–615**
    launch sites **5:392–394**
    launch vehicles
        5:395–397; **9**:662
    Saturn V **5**:392, 393,
        396–397; **8**:*610*
roll **4**:*282*, 285
ROVs *see* remotely
    operated vehicles
rudders
    aircraft **4**:286
    ship **9**:645

Sₐddles **1**:38
sailing **8:618–621**
St. Lawrence Seaway **2**:118,
    119
Sakigake (space probe)
    9:669
Salyut space stations
    9:670–671
satellites **8:622–625**;
    9:674–675
    astronomical **8**:624
    communications **3**:*167*;

Volume numbers are in **boldface type** followed by colons. Page numbers in **boldface type** refer to main articles and their illustrations; page numbers in *italic type* refer to picture captions.

8:622–623, *624*, 625; **10**:727
control systems **8**:622–623
and the Global Positioning System **5**:*328*–329; **7**:495; **8**:625
laser-powered microsatellites **5**:391
launch vehicles **5**:*395*–397; **8**:622
military **8**:624–625; **9**:692–693
orbits **5**:395; **8**:622, *624*
power systems **8**:623–624
remote-sensing **8**:624
rocket motors **8**:615
weather **6**:451; **8**:622, 624
Saturn, space probes to **9**:*663*, 666, 668, 669
Saturn V rockets **5**:392, 393, *396*–*397*; **8**:*610*, 615
scooters, motor **6**:471
scuba diving **3**:*192*, 193
seaplanes **8**:626
seiners **4**:*279*, 280
semitrailers **10**:754, *755*
sextants **5**:328; **7**:493
Shepard, Alan **9**:675
ships and boats **8**:634–638
aircraft carriers **1**:24–25; **6**:423
building **8**:636–638
bulk carriers **6**:*423*; **7**:554
canal boats **2**:119
cargo **7**:554–555
container ships **6**:*423*; **7**:554; **8**:*634*
cruise ships **7**:555
design **8**:635–636
drill ships **7**:507
fastest **8**:564–565
fishing vessels **4**:*278*–*279*, *280*, *281*
hovercraft **5**:*354*–*355*
hydrofoils **5**:*360*–*361*
icebreakers **9**:650
launching **8**:637

measuring speed of **7**:495
propellers **2**:*123*; **9**:644
rudders **9**:645
sailing **8**:618–621
tankers **2**:*123*; **7**:514–515, 551
tug boats **7**:552
see also navigation; ports
shock absorbers **1**:62, 63
Sikorsky, Igor **5**:343, *344*
skates, ice **9**:649
skiboards **9**:649
skiffs **8**:564
skis **9**:648–649
Skylab (space station) **9**:*671*
sleds **1**:37; **9**:*649*
sleighs **9**:649
snowblowers **9**:650
snowcats **9**:*650*
snowmobiles **9**:650; **10**:750
snowplows **9**:650
snowshoes **9**:*648*
snow travel **1**:37; **7**:502, *503*; **9**:*648*–*650*; **10**:750
Sojourner Rover (robot) **8**:*609*
solar wind, solar sails using **9**:664
sonic booms **1**:18, *19*
space flight **9**:662–664
space ports *see* launch sites
space probes **9**:662–663, **665**–**669**
space shuttles **9**:662, 670, *674*, 676–677
launching **5**:*393*–*394*, 397; **9**:662, *676*
propellants **4**:*303*, 305
reentry **9**:664, *676*
tiles **2**:*130*, 131
space stations **8**:625; **9**:670–673
International Space Station **4**:*252*; **8**:625; **9**:*672*–673
space suits **9**:663, *664*, 677–678
space travel **9**:674–679

rockets for **8**:611–612, 613, *614*–615
see also space probes; space shuttles
space walks **9**:677–678
spark plugs **1**:57; **4**:249, 251; **5**:*363*
speedometers **10**:753
Sperry, Elmer **7**:495
spoilers **8**:577
Sprinter 308E (electric vehicle) **3**:*223*
Spruce Goose (flying boat) **8**:626
stabilizer bars **1**:63
stalling, aircraft **4**:*283*, 284–285
Stardust (space probe) **9**:669
stealth aircraft **1**:26, 28; **3**:229; **4**:287; **8**:578
steam engines **4**:248–249, *250*; **9**:**682**–**687**, 712
for road vehicles **9**:686–687
for ships and boats **6**:421–422; **8**:564; **9**:*685*, *686*, 687
in steam locomotives **8**:587; **9**:*682*
world's first **2**:92
steering
automobiles **1**:59, **60**–**61**
power **1**:61
tanks **10**:749
Stephenson, George **8**:587
Stevens, Robert L. **8**:589–590
stock cars **8**:577
streamlining **1**:*17*, 18
streetcars **9**:694
submarines **9**:695–697
miniature **9**:696

nuclear **6**:*421*, 423; **7**:499; **9**:696, *697*
submersibles **3**:*193*, *195*; **9**:696
subway systems **8**:587; **9**:**698**–**701**
driverless trains **8**:607
Suez Canal **2**:*115*
Suisei (space probe) **9**:669
Sun, navigation by **7**:493
supercarriers **1**:25
supertankers **2**:*123*; **7**:515, 551
offshore moorings **7**:513
Surveyor space probes **9**:666
suspension systems
automobile **1**:62–63
bicycle **1**:78
switch engines **8**:586

Tankers **2**:*123*; **7**:514–515, 551
offshore moorings **7**:513
tanks **7**:502
and antitank shells **2**:95
Tereshkova, Valentina **9**:675
tetraethyl lead **4**:309
TGVs (*trains à grande vitesse*) **8**:588
throttle **4**:251
thrust **4**:282–283, 311
tie rods **1**:61
tillers **9**:645
tires **8**:617; **10**:746
automobile **1**:59; **8**:617; **10**:761, 789
pneumatic **1**:76; **10**:746
racing **8**:577

Tomahawk Cruise missiles are like small pilotless airplanes.

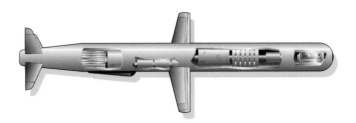

Titanic (ship) **8**:638
Titan rockets **5**:396
Tom Thumb (locomotive)
   8:590
Top Fuel cars **8**:577
torsion bars **1**:62, *63*
Tour de France **1**:77
tracked vehicles
   10:748–750
  for snow **9**:*650*; **10**:750
tractors (farming) **7**:502;
   10:748, **751–752**
  see also tracked vehicles
tractors (parts of trucks)
   10:754–*755*
trains
  cog railroads **2:157–158**
  diesel **8**:587–588
  driverless **8**:588, *607*
  electric **6**:427; **8**:*588*
  freight **8**:585–586, 588,
   593
  high-speed electric **6**:427;
   8:*588*

light-rail systems **8**:587,
   607; **9**:700
maglev **6**:*418*, 419
railroad cars **8:585–588**
railroad locomotives
   8:587–588
  steam **8**:587; **9**:*682*
  subway **8**:607; **9**:700
  tunnels **10:756–757**
  see also railroads
trawlers **4**:*279, 280, 281*
Trevithick, Richard **8**:587;
   9:686
trucks **10:754–755**
  brakes **2**:97
Tsiolkovsky, Konstantin
   8:612; **9**:675
tug boats **7**:552

Turbinia (steam boat) **9**:687
Turbosails **6**:422

U-boats **9**:695
unpiloted aerial vehicles
   (UAVs) *see* drone
   aircraft; robotic
   flight

Vega space probes **9**:667
Venera space probes
   9:666–667
Venus, space probes to
   9:*666–667*
Viking space probes **9**:667
vortex generators **4**:284–285
Voyager space probes **9**:*663,
   666*

VS-100 (helicopter) **5**:343
V/STOL aircraft **1**:25

Water jets, for marine
   propulsion **6**:422
water transport *see* canals,
   ship and boat
weightlessness, in space
   9:662, 664
Westinghouse, George
   8:585; **9**:687
wheels **1**:37; **9**:710;
   10:788–789
Wise, John **1**:66
Woolf, Arthur **9**:687
Wright, Orville and Wilbur
   1:30; **4**:286; **6**:427;
   9:713

Yachts **8**:619
yaw **4**:*282, 285*
Young, Arthur **5**:344

Zeppelins **1**:*67*

Volume numbers are in **boldface type** followed by colons. Page numbers in **boldface type** refer to main articles and their illustrations; page numbers in *italic type* refer to picture captions.

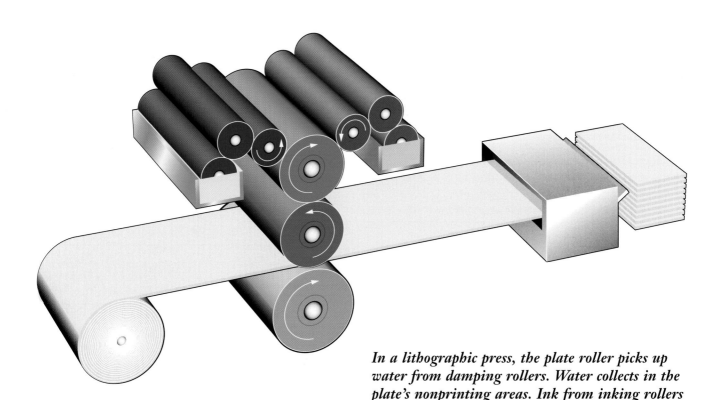

In a lithographic press, the plate roller picks up water from damping rollers. Water collects in the plate's nonprinting areas. Ink from inking rollers accumulates in printing areas. The ink image then transfers first to the roller and then to the paper.

General Index

A-4 rockets **8**:613
Aaron Manby (ship) **8**:636
Abbe, Ernst **5**:326
abrasives **1**:12–13
absolute temperature scale
  10:741–742
absolute zero **8**:596; **10**:742
AC *see* alternating current
acceleration, due to gravity
  6:431
accelerometers **6**:452
Acela trains **6**:427
acetate rayon **4**:270
Acheson, Edward Goodrich
  1:12
acid rain **2**:154; **7**:*549, 550*;
  8:567
acids **2**:140–141
Ackerman system **1**:61
acoustics **1**:14–15
  see also musical
    instruments; sound
    recording
actuators **6**:452
Ada, Countess of Lovelace
  3:174
adhesives **1**:16
adzes **5**:331
aeolipiles **9**:685
aerials *see* antennae
aerodynamics **1**:17–19
agonists **7**:532–533
agriculture **1**:20–21
  birth of **9**:710
  farm storage **4**:261
  fertilizers **1**:*21*;
    4:*264–265*; **7**:551
  livestock farming
    6:412–413
  organic farming
    7:518–519
  plow **7**:547
  sustainable farming **7**:519
  see also crops farming;

horticulture, pest
  control
AIDS **5**:366
ailerons **4**:286; **5**:327
air *see* atmosphere
airbags **1**:59; **6**:*452*
air conditioning **1**:22–23
  see also heating systems
aircraft
  airliners **1**: *27, 28*
  airships 1:66, *67*
  autopilots **7**:*494*
  balloons **1**:66–67
  brakes **2**:97
  construction 1:26–27, *29*
  control systems 1:28–29
  crop-spraying **3**:*186*, 187
  delta-winged **4**:287
  design **1**:26–29; **4**:287
  detection using radar
    8:*578, 579*
  displays on cockpit
    windows **5**:347
  electronic
    countermeasures
    3:*229*
  engines 1:27, 28, **30**;
    4:311
  flight **1**:18, *19*; **4**:282–287
  gliders **5**:327
  helicopters **5**:342-344
  jet 1:28; 4:287, 311; **6**:428
  main components 1:*29*
  micromachines and **6**:452
  missiles **6**:467
  paint 7:*521*
  pilotless 1:27; **8**:*606*–607
  seaplanes **8**:626

sonic booms **1**:18, *19*
stealth **1**:*26*, 28; **3**:229;
  4:287; **8**:578
"super jumbo" **1**:27
tires **8**:617
V/STOL **1**:25
see also aerodynamics;
  airports and airfields
aircraft carriers **1**:24–25;
  6:423
air-cushion vehicles *see*
  hovercraft
airliners **1**:27, 28
airports and airfields
  1:31–33; **2**:143
  airport surveillance radar
    (ASR) **8**:579
  automated people movers
    (APMs) **8**:607
  security 1:33; **8**:628–629,
    630
airships **1**:66, *67*
air-traffic control **1**:33
Akashi-Kaikyo Bridge **2**:107
alarms, intruder **8**:628
alcohol, as a fuel **4**:*305*
algal blooms **7**:551
alkalis **2**:141
alkylation **7**:513–514
allergies **5**:*365*, 366
alloys **1**:34
all-terrain vehicles (ATVs)
  . . **7**:503
alpha particles and alpha
  decay **7**:497;
  8:580–581
Altair 8800 (computer)
  3:174

alternating current (AC)
  3:213, 218, 219–220
  AC generators **3**:*221*
  AC motors **3**:221–222
alternative therapies **7**:530
alternators **3**:222; **4**:251
ALU (arithmetic-logic unit)
  3:172
aluminum **6**:444, 446
  abundance **7**:517
  aircraft construction
    1:28
  production **3**:225
  recycling **10**:773
Alvin (submersible) **3**:195
Alzheimer's disease **7**:530
amalgams **6**:447
  dental **3**:198–199
ammonia **2**:141
  and fertilizers **4**:265
  production **2**:125, 140
ammonium nitrate-fuel oil
  mixtures (ANFOs)
  4:258
Ampère, André-Marie
  6:419
amphibious vehicles **7**:*502*,
  503
Amphicars **7**:503
ampicillin **1**:44
amplifiers **1**:35; **5**:370
analgesics **7**:533
analog technology **3**:206
  analog electronics **3**:232,
    233
  analog to digital
    conversion **3**:206
anemia **7**:531
anemometers **6**:450–*451*
anesthetics **6**:*441*; **9**:704,
  705
ANFOs (ammonium
  nitrate-fuel oil
  mixtures) **4**:258

Volume numbers are in **boldface type** followed by colons. Page numbers in **boldface type** refer to main articles and their illustrations; page numbers in *italic type* refer to picture captions.

angiography **6**:434

angioscopes **3**:238

animal breeding **1:36**
  selective breeding **1**:36; **3**:188
  see also cloning; livestock farming

animals, treatment of *see* veterinary medicine

animal transportation **1:37–38**; **9**:*649*

animation **1:39–41**
  see also moviemaking

antennae **1:42–43**; **8**:584
  television **10**:732, *733*

anthracite **2**:153; **4**:304

anthrax **2**:133

antibiotics **1:44–45**; **2**:139; **6**:440; **7**:532

antibodies **5**:364–365
  and cancer **2**:121

antidepressants **7**:534

antilock braking system (ABS) **2**:97

antipsychotic drugs **7**:534

antiseptics **1:46–47**; **7**:531; **9**:704
  see also surgery

aphids **2**:*84*; **7**:*528*

APMs (automated people movers) **8**:607

Apollo space program **9**:675–676

appendectomy **9**:705, 706

applets **9**:653

aquaculture **1:48–49**
  see also fishing industry

aqualungs **3**:193

aqueducts **2**:*104*, 116

aquifers **5**:385; **7**:551

archeology **1:50–51**

Archimedes **3**:181, 183

Archimedes screw **3**:181

Archimedes wave swings (AWSs) **10**:785

argon **4**:308

Ariane rockets **5**:397

arithmetic-logic unit (ALU) **3**:172

armor **1**:38

arms, artificial **2**:87

arthritis, rheumatoid **5**:366; **7**:530

artificial intelligence **1:52–54**

ASCII code **3**:172

asphalt **8**:602, 603

Aspidin, Joseph **2**:127

aspirin **7**:532

assembly lines **1**:*58*

astrolabes **7**:493

Aswan Dam **5**:*358*

ATC (automatic train control) systems **8**:593–594

Atlantis (space shuttle) **9**:*670*, *674*

atmosphere, gases **4**:307

ATMs (automated teller machines) **1**:*69*

atomic energy *see* nuclear energy

atoms **2**:139; **3**:212; **7**:*490*, 496

Attack Laser program **5**:391

attrition **1**:12

ATVs (all-terrain vehicles) **7**:503

augers **3**:181

autoclaves **1**:47

autogiros **5**:344

autoimmunity **5**:365–366

automated people movers (APMs) **8**:607

automated teller machines (ATMs) **1**:*69*

automatic train control (ATC) systems **8**:593–594

automobiles **1:55–59**
  aerodynamics **1**:*18*, 19
  brake lights **3**:201
  brake systems **1**:59; **2**:96–97; **5**:*357*
  computers on **1**:57
  cooling **1**:58; **5**:337
  design **1**:19, *57*
  electric **3**:223
  electrical system **1**:59, 71; **5**:362–363
  engine **1**:57–58; **5**:362
  exhaust systems **1**:57–58
  first **1**:55; **5**:*376*, 377
  four-wheel drive **1**:59
  fuel **4**:309
  fuel intake systems **1**:57
  hybrid **3**:223
  ignition systems **1**:57; **5**:362–*363*
  instrument panel **10**:753
  lubrication **1**:58
  manufacture **1**:56, *58*
  safety systems **1**:59
  steering **1**:59, **60–61**
  suspension **1:62–63**
  tires **1**:59; **8**:617; **10**:761, 789
  transmission systems **1**:57; **4**:*313*; **5**:*357*; **6**:429–430
  wheels **1**:59, 60
  see also race cars

autonomous underwater vehicles (AUVs) **3**:195

autopilots **7**:*494*

autopsies **4**:296; **9**:703

Auto Train **8**:587

AUVs (autonomous underwater vehicles) **3**:195

auxins **5**:351

AWACS aircraft **4**:*283*

AWSs (Archimedes wave swings) **10**:785

Aztecs **9**:712

Babbage, Charles **3**:174

babbitt metal **6**:430

Bacillus thuringiensis **2**:85

backhoes **3**:179, *180*

bacteria
  antibiotics **1**:44, 45
  antiseptics **1**:46–47
  biological control **2**:85
  biotechnology **2**:88, *89*, *90*
  pollution **2**:90; **7**:551
  see also Escherichia coli

bagpipes **7**:487

Baird, John Logie **10**:*735*

Bakelite **7**:542

baking industry **1:64–65**

balances **10**:*786–787*

Ballistic Missile Early Warning System (BMEWS) **9**:692

balloon framing **2**:108

balloons **1:66–67**

banking **1:68–69**
  security **8**:629–630

Banting, Frederick Grant **7**:534

barber-surgeons **9**:703

bar codes **5**:*367*; **8**:599

Bardeen, John **3**:230, 232

barges **2**:119

barometers **6**:450

Barton, Otis **3**:194

base transceiver stations (BTSs) **10**:*726*, 727

BASIC (computer language) **3**:174; **9**:652

Bassi, Agostino **1**:44

bassoons **7**:488

bathyspheres **3**:194

batteries **1:70–71**; **3**:213–214; **5**:362

Battleship Potemkin (film) **6**:475

Baudot, Emile **10**:724

Bauhaus **3**:201–202

Baylis, Trevor **5**:*375*

B-cells **5**:365

Beams, Jesse **2**:129

Volume numbers are in **boldface type** followed by colons. Page numbers in **boldface type** refer to main articles and their illustrations; page numbers in *italic type* refer to picture captions.

beams, cantilever
    9:646–647
bearings 4:262; 6:430
Becquerel, Antoine-César
    9:655
Becquerel, Henri 7:497
Beebe, Charles 3:194
beer 2:88, 89, 90, 98–99
Behrens, Peter 3:200–201
Bell, Alexander Graham
    5:360; 9:714–715,
    716; 10:725
Bell Model 47 (helicopter)
    5:344
bends, the 3:192–193
benzene 2:155
Benz, Karl 1:55; 5:377
Berliner, Emile 9:658
Bernard, Claude 7:532
Berners-Lee, Tim 5:374
Bernouilli effect 4:282
Bessemer, Henry 5:379,
    380; 9:712–713
Best, Charles H. 7:534
beta particles and beta
    decay 1:70; 7:497;
    8:581
beverages 1:72–75
    beer 2:88, 89, 90, 98–99
    cocoa 1:73
    coffee 1:72–73, 75; 4:289
    fruit juices 1:75
    spirits 1:74–75
    tea 1:72; 3:184
bicycles 1:76–78
    brakes 1:77–78; 2:96
    streamlined 1:17
    tires 10:746
    transmission system and
        gears 1:76–77, 78;
        6:429, 430
bimetallic strips 10:742
binary code 3:170, 207;
    5:367; 9:688
    compact discs (CDs)
        3:168–169;
        5:390–391; 9:689
    computer graphics
        3:176–177

fax machines 4:260
fiber optics 4:267
binoculars 6:405–406
biofuels 4:305
biological control 2:84–85
biological weapons see
    chemical and germ
    warfare
bionics (biomedical
    engineering) 2:86–87;
    4:255; 6:443
biopsies 3:205; 9:704
bioreactors 2:88, 89
biosensors 2:90; 6:439
biotechnology 2:88–90
    genetic engineering 1:36;
        2:89; 4:314–316;
        7:529
Birdseye, Clarence 4:289
birth control 7:534
Birth of a Nation (film)
    6:475
bitmap (BMP) files 3:177
Black Death 10:765
blackfly, citrus 3:187
black powder 4:272; 8:610
blanching, food 4:288, 291
blast furnaces 2:91–92;
    5:379, 381–382
bleaches 2:147
blood
    cells 5:364
    forensic science and 4:298
    tests 3:204
    transfusions 2:93
bloodletting 9:703
blood pressure 3:204; 6:439
    high 7:534
Blucher (locomotive) 8:587
BMEWS (Ballistic Missile
    Early Warning
    System) 9:692
boats see ships and boats
bobsledding 9:649
boilers, steam engine 9:682,
    683
bolts 4:263
Boltwood, Bertram 7:497
bombs and shells 2:94–95

"smart" bombs 6:468
see also missiles; nuclear
    weapons; torpedoes
    and depth charges
bone marrow, transplants
    5:366
boreholes 6:461
borescopes 3:238
boring mills 6:416–417
bourbon 1:75
bovine growth hormone
    (BST) 3:188
braces, teeth 3:199
brain, electroencephalo-
    grams (EEGs) 6:440
brake lights 3:201
brake systems 2:96–97
    automobile 1:59; 2:96–97;
        5:357
    bicycle 1:77–78; 2:96
    motorcycle 6:472
    railroad car 8:585
brand identity 3:201
brandy 1:75
Branson, Richard 1:67
Brattain, Walter 3:230
bread, making 1:64–65
breakwaters 2:143
breeding
    animal see animal
        breeding
    plant 5:349–350
see also livestock farming
Breitling Orbiter 3 (balloon)
    1:67

brewing industry 2:98–99
see also beverages
bricks and masonry
    2:100–101, 109, 110
bridges 2:102–107
    Akashi-Kaikyo Bridge
        2:107
    arch 2:103, 104–105;
        4:254
    Bailey Island Bridge
        2:103
    beam 2:103–104
    bridging tanks 10:750
    Brooklyn Bridge 2:106
    cable-stayed 2:107
    cantilever 2:103, 105–106
    cement and concrete for
        2:102–103
    clapper 2:103
    Confederation Bridge
        2:107
    drawbridges 2:107
    iron and steel for
        2:102–103, 106, 107,
        112
    moveable 2:107
    Oresund Bridge 2:107
    pontoon 2:103
    Quebec Bridge 2:105
    Seto-Ohashi Bridge 2:107

*In an overshot
waterwheel, the water
that turns the wheel
enters from the top.*

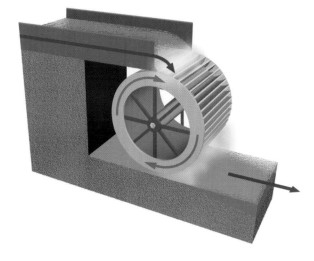

bridges (*cont*)
  suspension **2**:*103*, 106, 107, 112
  Sunshine Skyway Bridge **2**:107
  Sydney Harbour Bridge **2**:105
  Tacoma Narrows Bridge **1**:18; **2**:106
  Tay Bridge disaster **2**:108
  truss **2**:104
Brindley, James **2**:143
Broglie, prince Louis de **6**:459
bronze **1**:34; **5**:330
Bronze Age **9**:710
Brooklyn Bridge **2**:106
brownouts **3**:217
Brunel, Isambard Kingdom **2**:110, 143, 144; **9**:698
Brunelleschi, Filippo **2**:110
BSE (mad cow disease) **6**:412
bubble chambers **8**:*581*
bucket wheels **5**:386
buckminsterfullerene **2**:141
Buenos Ayrean (ship) **8**:636
buggies, dune **7**:503
buildings
  aerodynamics and **1**:19
  building techniques **2**:**108–112**
  demolition **3**:*196*–197
  foundations **4**:302
  see also bricks and masonry; cement and concrete; civil engineering; elevator; skyscrapers
bulk carriers **6**:*423*; **7**:554
bulldozers **3**:179, 180
bullets **4**:273
  forensic science and **4**:297
buoys **6**:409; **7**:553–554
buses **2**:**113**
butadiene **8**:617
butterfly effect (chaos theory) **2**:132
bytes **9**:688

Cable cars **2**:158
cables, electrical **2**:**114**
cableways **2**:158
CAD *see* computer-aided design
caissons **2**:118–119; **4**:302; **6**:409
cakes and cookies **1**:65
calendering machines **10**:740
calorific value **4**:304
calorimeters **4**:304
camels **1**:*37*
cameras **7**:536–539
  digital **3**:*207*; **7**:*537*
  movie **6**:473–474, 476–*477*, 478
  security cameras **8**:*628*
  television **10**:734
Cameron, James **6**:*473*
canals **2**:**115–119**
  building **2**:115–116
  elevators **2**:119; **3**:237
cancer
  causes **2**:120
  treatments **2**:**120–121**; **6**:440
candles **6**:410
canning **4**:289
canoes, dugout **8**:634, *635*
cans
  drink **3**:202
  tin **3**:225
capacitors **3**:216, 217; **6**:455
  in electronic circuits **3**:231, *233*
Cape Canaveral **5**:392, *393*
  demolition at **3**:197
carbohydrates **4**:294
carbon
  isotopes **7**:496, 497
  radiocarbon dating **1**:51; **7**:497

carbon dioxide, and global warming **4**:245, *246–247*, 305; **8**:568
carbon fiber **1**:76
carbon steel **6**:416
carborundum **1**:12
carburetors **4**:251
cargo
  air **1**:33
  ships' **7**:*554–555*
Carnegie, Andrew **5**:383
Carothers, Wallace **4**:270, 271, 279
carrots **7**:519
Carson, Rachel **7**:528
cartoons **1**:39
cartridges, firearm **4**:272–273
carvel construction **8**:636
case hardening **6**:449
cash registers **8**:598–599
cassettes, tape **9**:659–660
Cassini (space probe) **9**:*669*
casting **2**:**122–123**; **6**:*446*, 448
Castner-Kellner process **3**:225
catalysts **2**:**124–125**, 135; **6**:446
  used in oil refining **7**:513–514
  see also chemical industry; enzymes
catalytic converters **1**:57–58; **2**:125
catamarans **8**:565
cathedrals, Gothic **2**:*109*, 110
cathode ray tubes **3**:*234*, 235; **10**:733, 735
CAT scans *see* computed tomography
"cat's eyes" **8**:602

cattle **6**:*412*
  dairy **3**:188–*189*; **6**:412
cauterization **9**:702
cavalry **1**:38
cavitation **5**:361; **9**:644
Caxton, William **8**:570
CCDs (charge-coupled devices) **7**:537; **8**:633; **10**:729, 766
CCTV (closed-circuit television) **8**:*627*, 628; **9**:717
CDs *see* compact discs
cells
  battery **1**:70–71
  biotechnology and **2**:88–89
  organelles **2**:129
cellular phones (cell phones)
  see telephony and telegraphy
celluloid **7**:545
cellulose **2**:139
  cellulose acetate **7**:545
  cellulose nitrate **7**:545
  fibers made from **4**:269, 270
Celsius temperature scale **10**:741
cement and concrete **2**:101, 111–112, **126–127**
  bridges **2**:102–103
  prestressed concrete **2**:127
  reinforced concrete **2**:102, 103, *111*, 127; **4**:302
  roads **8**:602
  see also building techniques
central heating **5**:339–341
centralized traffic control (CTC) **8**:594
central processing unit (CPU) **3**:170–172
centrifugal force **2**:128
centrifuges **2**:**128–129**
ceramics **2**:**130–131**
  abrasive **1**:13
  see also pottery

Volume numbers are in **boldface type** followed by colons. Page numbers in **boldface type** refer to main articles and their illustrations; page numbers in *italic type* refer to picture captions.

cesium atomic clocks **10**:745

CFCs *see* chlorofluorocarbons

chain reaction **7**:498–499, 500–501

Challenger (space shuttle) **5**:397; **9**:676

Champ racing **8**:576

Channel Tunnel **5**:329; **10**:757

chaos theory **2**:132

charcoal **2**:91

Chardonnet, Louis-Marie-Hilaire Bernigaud, Count of **4**:270

charge-coupled devices (CCDs) **7**:537; **8**:633; **10**:729, 766

cheese **3**:189; **4**:292

chemical engineering **2**:134–136; **4**:253
see also chemical industry

chemical and germ warfare **2**:133

chemical industry **2**:137–141
see also chemical engineering; oil and natural gas

chemicals
inorganic **2**:139–141
organic **2**:137–139
see also chemical engineering

chemigation **3**:187

chemotherapy **2**:121; **6**:440

Chernobyl disaster **2**:144; **7**:498, 548

chess, computers playing **1**:52, 54

chickens **6**:413

chimneys, factory, demolition **3**:197

China, ancient **9**:711

chips *see* integrated circuits

chisels **5**:331; **10**:798

chlorhexidine **10**:764

chlorine, isotopes **2**:129

chlorofluorocarbons (CFCs) **4**:308; **7**:550; **8**:596
and nanomachines **7**:491

chloroform **6**:441

chromatography, gas **4**:298

chromosomes **4**:314

chronometers **5**:328; **7**:493, 494–495

Cierva, Juan de la **5**:343, 344

CIM (computer-integrated manufacture) **3**:202

cinchona **7**:531–532

ciphers **2**:156

circuit boards **3**:231

circuit breakers **3**:218

circuit switching **3**:166

civil engineering **2**:142–145; **4**:252–253, 254
railroad construction **8**:589–591
roads **8**:600–605
see also bridges; skyscrapers; surveying; tunnels

Civil War **4**:272, 274
balloons **1**:66
iron ships **8**:636

clarinets **7**:487, 488

clay **2**:100; **7**:556, 557–558

cleaning agents **2**:146–147

Clementine (space probe) **9**:666

clinker boats **8**:636

clocks and watches **10**:743–745
atomic clocks **5**:329; **10**:745
digital **3**:206; **10**:745
electric **10**:744–745
mechanical **10**:744

cloning **1**:36; **2**:148–149

clothing, firefighting **4**:277

clothing industry **2**:150–152
see also fibers and yarns; manufacture; textiles

cloud chambers **8**:581

coal **2**:153–155; **4**:245, 304
brown (lignite) **2**:153, 154; **4**:304
mining **2**:153; **6**:464, 465
pollution **4**:246
use in power stations **2**:155; **8**:567

coal gas (town gas) **4**:304, 306
use in power stations **2**:155

coal tar **2**:138, 155

coastal engineering **2**:143

cobalt-60 **4**:289

cochineal **3**:210

cochlear implants **2**:87

Cockerell, Christopher **5**:354

Cockerell's rafts **10**:785

cocoa **1**:73

coconuts, fibers from **4**:270

codes and ciphers **2**:156
radio encryption **9**:716
see also binary code; information theory; Morse code

coffee **1**:72–73, 75; **4**:289

cog railroads **2**:157–158

coins **1**:68

coke **2**:154, 155; **4**:304; **7**:517
in iron production **5**:380

color **3**:164–165

and computer graphics **3**:176–177

Colosseum **2**:111–112, 127

Colt .45 (revolver) **4**:273

combine harvesters **5**:332–333; **6**:428

combustion **4**:257, 303–304

communication networks **3**:166–167
and satellites **3**:167; **8**:622–623, 624, 625
see also cellular phones telephony and telegraphy

compact discs **3**:168–169; **5**:390–391; **8**:633; **9**:660, 689
CD-ROMs **3**:168, 169; **7**:484, 485
CD-Rs (CD-rewriteable discs) **3**:169, 174; **9**:689
see also digital versatile discs; minidiscs

compactors **3**:179

companion planting **7**:519, 527

compasses **6**:418; **7**:493–494

Light rays from a candle are reflected in a mirror. The rays are bent before entering the eye.

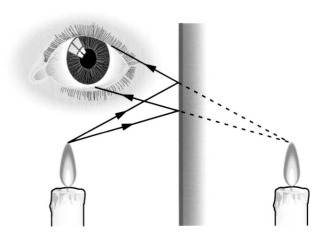

composites, in aircraft construction **1**:28

composting **10**:774

computed tomography (computerized axial tomography) **3**:205; **6**:435, 439

computer-aided design (CAD) **3**:*203*
for aircraft **1**:26
for clothing **2**:150, 151
for machine tools **6**:417

computer graphics **3**:**176–177**

computer-integrated manufacture (CIM) **3**:202

computerized axial tomography *see* computed tomography

computers **3**:**170–175**
arithmetic-logic unit (ALU) **3**:172
central processing unit (CPU) **3**:170–172
disks and drives **3**:168, 169, 173–174; **9**:688–689
ENIAC **3**:174
graphical user interface (GUI) **3**:177; **9**:653
keyboard **3**:172
languages **9**:652
laptop **10**:733–734
medicine **6**:439
memory **3**:172–173
monitors **6**:420; **10**:733
nanocomputers **7**:491
networks **3**:167; **9**:717–718
operating system **3**:170
palmtop *see* personal digital assistants
personal (PCs) **3**:174–175, *202*; **7**:484–485
processing speed (clock speed) **3**:172
quantum **8**:633
run using lasers **5**:391
security **8**:630
software *see* software and programming
viruses **8**:630
voice recognition **10**:769
see also artificial intelligence; Internet; personal digital assistants

Comuta (car) **3**:223

Concorde (aircraft) **1**:*27*

concrete *see* cement and concrete

conduction (heat) **5**:338, 339, 368

conductors, electrical **3**:213

Confederation Bridge **2**:107

Congreve, William **6**:466

construction sites **3**:**178–180**

containers **8**:586, *634*

Contour (space probe) **9**:669

convection **5**:338, 339

conveyors **3**:**181**; **6**:429

Cooke, William **10**:724

cookies **1**:*65*

copper **6**:446
ores **7**:516, 517

coppicing **4**:299–300

Corinth Canal **2**:*117*, 118

corrosion **3**:**182**

Cort, Henry **5**:380

cosmeses **2**:87

cotton **4**:*268*, 269–270; **9**:713; **10**:738
see also textiles

cotton gins **9**:713

Courtelle **4**:271

Cousteau, Jacques **3**:193

CPU (central processing unit) **3**:170–172

crabs, fishing for **4**:280–281

cracking **2**:125; **7**:510–511, *512*, 513

cranes **3**:*183*; **7**:554

crankshafts **4**:248–249

crawlers **10**:748, 750, 751

credit cards, holograms **5**:347

creosote **7**:521

Crookes, William **8**:583

crops
cash **3**:184
farming **3**:**184–185**; **5**:351; **9**:654
genetically-engineered **4**:314–315; **7**:529
irrigation **5**:**384–387**; **10**:778
rotation **7**:519
spraying **3**:**186–187**
storage **4**:261
see also agriculture; fertilizers; harvesting machinery; horticulture; pesticides and herbicides; plows; tractors

cross staffs **7**:493

crowns, dental **3**:199

crude oil *see* oil and natural gas

cryogenics **8**:596

cryosurgery **6**:442

cryptograms **2**:156

Crystal Palace **2**:110–111

CT *see* computed tomography

CTC (centralized traffic control) **8**:594

Cugnot, Nicolas-Joseph **9**:686

cultivators (harrows) **3**:184

curare **7**:532

cuttings, plant **5**:351

cyclohexane **2**:*136*

Dacron **4**:271; **9**:678

Daimler, Gottlieb **1**:55; **5**:*376*, 377

dairy industry **3**:**188–189**

Dalton, John **2**:139, 140

dams **3**:**190–191**; **5**:*358–359*; **10**:776, *781*
Grand Coulee Dam **5**:359
Hoover Dam **3**:*190*, 191
Itaipu Dam **2**:*145*
South Fork Dam **3**:191
Vaiont Dam **3**:191

Darby, Abraham **5**:379–380; **9**:712

Darrieus turbines **10**:759

DATs (digital audio tapes) **9**:660

Davy, Sir Humphry **3**:225; **6**:410–411

Dawn (space probe) **9**:667

DC *see* direct current

DDT **3**:187; **7**:528, 529

deaf people, cochlear implants **2**:87

debris, space **8**:623

Deep Blue (computer) **1**:54

deep-sea technology **3**:**192–195**

Deep Space 1 (space probe) **9**:668–669

defibrillators **6**:443

deflagration **4**:257

deforestation **4**:301

De Forest, Lee **3**:230; **6**:476; **9**:716; **10**:736, 794

demolition **3**:**196–197**

dendrochronology **1**:*51*

dentistry **3**:**198–199**
drills **1**:*13*

dentures **3**:199

depth charges **10**:747

derricks **3**:183

design, industrial **3**:**200–203**

Volume numbers are in **boldface type** followed by colons. Page numbers in **boldface type** refer to main articles and their illustrations; page numbers in *italic type* refer to picture captions.

desktop publishing (DTP) **8**:571, 573

detergents **2**:146–*147*

detonation **4**:257

deuterium **7**:501

dhows **8**:621

diabetes **6**:439; **7**:534

diagnostic equipment **3**:**204–205**

see also medical imaging

dialysis **6**:443

diamonds **1**:12, *13*

synthetic **1**:12, 13

Dickinson, John **7**:523

diesel engines *see* engines, diesel

diffraction **6**:406; **10**:783

diggers **10**:*750*

digital audio tapes (DATs) **9**:660

digitalis **7**:*532*

digital technology **3**:**206–207**; **9**:717

electronics **3**:232–233

radio **8**:584; **10**:795

sound recording **9**:660

telephone signals **3**:166–167; **10**:725–72

television **3**:207; **10**:736

video **10**:767–768

see also computer; digital versatile discs

digital versatile discs (DVDs) **3**:168, 169, 174; **8**:633; **9**:689; **10**:766, 768

and multimedia **7**:*484, 485*

see also digital technology

dikes **2**:143; **3**:191; **10**:781

diodes **3**:231, *233*, 234, *235*; **8**:633; **10**:735

light-emitting (LEDs) **3**:231; **4**:267

Dioscorides **7**:531

direct current (DC) **3**:218, 219

DC generators **3**:*221*

DC motors **3**:*220*, 221

discharge tubes, fluorescent **6**:411

Discovery (space shuttle) **5**:*394*

disease(s)

animal **10**:764–765

the immune system and *see* immunology

dishwashers **10**:*771*

disinfectants **1**:*46, 47*

Disney, Walt **1**:39

distance, measured using lasers **5**:391

distillation

fractional **7**:512

of salt water **10**:779

of spirits **1**:74

vacuum **7**:512

distributors **5**:363

diving, underwater **3**:*192–193, 192–195*

diving bells **3**:193, 194

DNA **4**:*314*

analysis **3**:205

DNA fingerprinting **4**:297, 315

genetic engineering and **2**:89; **4**:314, *315*, 316

nanotechnology **7**:491

recombinant **4**:314, *316*

DNA ligase **4**:314

Docklands Light Railway **8**:*607*

dogsledding **9**:*649*

see also animal transportation

Dolby system **9**:660, 661

Dolly (sheep) **2**:*148*, 149

domain names **5**:372

domes **4**:*255*

donkeys **1**:37, 38

doping **4**:267; **8**:632–633

drag **1**:17; **4**:*283*

draglines **6**:463

drag racing **8**:577

drainage, land **5**:387

drawbridges **2**:107

drawing, metals **6**:448–449

dredging **3**:**208–209**

drilling, seeds **3**:184

drills **5**:331

electric **5**:*331*

drinks *see* beverages

drivers, printer **8**:574

drone aircraft **1**:27; **8**:607

drugs, therapeutic *see* antibiotics; pharmacology

drums **7**:489

dry cleaning **2**:147

drying, food **4**:289

DSL (Digital Subscriber Line) **5**:374

Dummer, Geoffrey **5**:370

Dunlop, John Boyd **1**:76; **8**:616; **10**:746

duplexers **8**:578

Duryea, Charles and James **1**:55

DVDs *see* digital versatile discs

dyes and dying **2**:138; **3**:165, **210–211**

mixing **3**:*165*

dynamite **4**:258

dynamometers **8**:619

dynamos **3**:222

Ears, cochlear implants **2**:87

earthenware **7**:557

earthquakes, and seismography **6**:461; **7**:505; **8**:631

Eastman, George **6**:473

ECGs (electrocardiograms) **6**:439–440

Ecostar (car) **3**:223

eddy currents **3**:222

Edison, Thomas Alva **3**:230; **6**:411, 474; **9**:658, 686, 712; **10**:724, 735

EDMs (electronic distance measuring devices) **9**:708

EEGs (electroencephalo-grams) **6**:440

Ehrlich, Paul **1**:44

EIAs (environmental impact assessments) **2**:145

Eiffel Tower **2**:111

Einstein, Albert **5**:390

Eisenstein, Sergei **6**:475

elastomers **8**:616

electricity **3**:**212–214**

electric circuits **3**:213–214, 231

electric current **3**:213–*214*, 230–231; **6**:445

for lighting **6**:410–*411*

static **3**:213

transmission **2**:114; **3**:**215–218**; **8**:566–567

electric motors **3**:**219–222**; **6**:420

synchronous **10**:744–745

electric road vehicles **3**:223

electrocardiograms (ECGs) **6**:439–440

electrochemical machining **6**:417

electrodes **1**:70

electroencephalograms (EEGs) **6**:440

electrolysis **2**:139–140; **3**:**224–225**

A pavement has four courses: the wearing course, base course, road base, and subbase.

electrolytes **1**:70–71; **3**:224
electromagnetic force **3**:212
electromagnetic (EM)
    waves,
        communication with
        1:42, 43
electromagnets **3**:221,
    226–227; **6**:418; **7**:516
    in loudspeakers **6**:*455*
    in televisions **6**:420;
        10:733
electromechanical devices
    3:226–228
electron beam machining
    6:417
electronic countermeasures
    3:229
electronic distance
    measuring devices
    (EDMs) **9**:708
electronic news gathering
    (ENG) **1**:43
electronics **3:230–233**
    see also amplifiers;
        electron tubes;
        integrated circuits;
        semiconductors
electrons
    and atom **7**:496
    and batteries **1**:71
    and electricity **3**:212–213,
        214
    and electrolysis **3**:224
    and light particles
        (photons) **5**:389
electron tubes **3:234–235**
electroplating **3**:*225*; **6**:449
elephants **1**:38
elevators (aircraft control
        surfaces) **4**:286
elevators (lifts) **2**:111;
    3:236–237; **9**:646
    canal **2**:119; **3**:237
    grain **4**:*261*
    see also escalators
Ely, Eugene **1**:25
e-mail **3**:175; **5**:374
Empire State Building
    9:*646*, 647

enamel, vitreous **7**:521
enantiomers **2**:*139*
encyclopedias, CD-ROM
    7:484, 485
endoscopes **3**:238; **6**:437,
    442–443; **9**:704
energy
    combustion and
        4:303–304
    conservation of **4**:245
    potential and kinetic
        4:245
    see also energy resources
energy resources
    4:244–247
    see also geothermal energy;
        hydroelectricity;
        nuclear energy; solar
        power; wave power;
        wind power
engineering **4:252–255**
    aerospace **4**:253
    biomedical (bionics)
        2:86–87; **4**:255
    chemical **2:134–136**;
        4:253
    civil *see* civil engineering
    coastal **2**:143
    electrical and electronics
        4:255
    environmental **2**:144;
        4:254
    genetic **1**:36; **2**:89;
        4:314–316; **7**:529
    marine **6:421–423**
    mechanical **6:426–428**
    military **4**:253
    nuclear **4**:254–255
engines **4:248–251**
    aircraft **1**:30
    automobile **1**:57–58;
        5:362
    ceramics used in **2**:131

diesel **2**:157; **4**:*251*; **5**:362;
    6:422, *423*; **8**:587–588
external combustion
    4:249, 311
gasoline **4**:*249*–250, 251
ignition systems
    5:362–363
in-line **1**:30
internal combustion
    4:249–251
ion **8**:615
jet **1**:30; **6**:*427*, 428
motorcycle **6**:471–472
outboard and inboard
    8:564
radial **1**:30
reciprocating **9**:683
rocket **5**:395, 396; **8**:*611*
rotary **1**:30; **9**:683
steam *see* steam engines
Stirling (gas engines)
    4:311
V-type **1**:30
    see also gas turbines and
        engines
ENIAC **3**:174
Enigma machines **2**:*156*
entomology, forensic **4**:297
Environmental Concept
    Buses (ECBs) **2**:113
environmental engineering
    2:144; **4**:254
environmental impact
    assessments (EIAs)
    2:145
enzymes **2**:90
    brewing and **2**:90, 98
    detergents **2**:147
    drugs affecting **7**:532
    genetic engineering and
        4:314
    restriction **4**:314
equator **7**:492

ergonomics **3**:200
erosion
    coastal **2**:143
    soil **9**:654
escalators **4**:256; **6**:429
    see also elevators
Escherichia coli (*E. coli*)
    and food poisoning **4**:294
    and genetic engineering
        2:89, *90*; **4**:314
etching, glass **1**:13
ether **6**:441
ethylene **5**:351; **7**:511
euro, the **1**:69
Evans, Oliver **9**:686
Evinrude, Ole **8**:564
excavators **3**:*178–180*;
    5:356; **6**:462
    draglines **6**:463
exhaust systems, automobile
    1:57–58
Exocet missiles **6**:467
expendable launch vehicles
    (ELVs) **5**:396
expert systems **1**:53
Explorer 1 (satellite) **9**:674
explosives **4:257–258**
    for demolition **3**:197
exposed location single
    buoy moorings
    (ELSBMs) **7**:513
extinguishers, fire **4**:*277*
extranets **5**:373
extravehicular mobility
    units (EMUs)
    9:677–678
extrusion **6**:*445*, 448; **7**:546
Exxon Valdez (ship) **7**:515
eyeglasses **6**:407, 459
eyes, laser surgery
    5:390–391

F-117 Nighthawk (stealth
    aircraft) **1**:*26*; **3**:229;
    4:287
facsimile transmission
    4:259–260
Faraday, Michael **3**:225;
    8:582; **10**:793

Volume numbers are in **boldface type** followed
by colons. Page numbers in **boldface type** refer to
main articles and their illustrations; page numbers in
italic type refer to picture captions.

Fahrenheit temperature scale **10**:741

farming *see* agriculture

farm storage **4**:261

farsightedness **6**:470

fastening and joining **4**:262–263

fat(s)
  body **4**:291
  processing **4**:291–292

fax machines *see* facsimile transmission

feet (units of measurement) **6**:425

felts **10**:739, 740

fermentation
  baking **1**:64, 65
  brewing **2**:98–99
  wine making **1**:73, 74

fermenters **2**:135–136

ferries
  hovercraft **5**:354
  hydrofoil **5**:361
  roll-on, roll-off **7**:554; **8**:637

fertilizers **1**:21; **4**:264–265; **7**:551

fiberglass **5**:368

fiber optics **3**:167; **4**:266–267; **5**:326, 391; **6**:406
  endoscopes **3**:238
  for telephone networks **9**:716; **10**:726

fiberscopes **3**:238

fibers and yarns **4**:268–271; **10**:738
  dyeing **3**:211
  see also textiles

field emission displays (FEDs) **3**:235

field-emission microscopes (FEMs) **6**:459

files (tools) **5**:331

film, photographic **7**:537–538, 539–541

films, animated *see* animation

filters, air **1**:47

fingerprinting **4**:296–297
  genetic **4**:297, 315

firearms **4**:272–274
  forensic science and **4**:297

firefighting **4**:275–277

fires, open **5**:339

fire trucks **4**:275, 276

"firewalls" **8**:630

fish
  farming *see* aquaculture
  stocks **4**:281

fishing industry **4**:278–281

fission, nuclear **4**:247; **7**:498, 500

flags **6**:424

flails **5**:332

flashlights **3**:213–214; **7**:540

flashovers **4**:277

flash point **4**:275

flatbeds **8**:586

flax **4**:269

Fleischer, Max **1**:39

Fleming, Alexander **1**:44, 45

Fleming, John Ambrose **10**:794

flight **1**:18, 19; **4**:282–287
  helicopter **5**:342
  robotic **8**:606–607
  space **9**:662–664
  see also aerodynamics; aircraft; balloons

flintlocks **4**:272

flipbooks **6**:473

Flixborough disaster **2**:136

floatplanes **8**:626

flood barriers **3**:191

floppy disks **3**:173; **9**:689

Florence, cathedral **2**:110

flotation, froth **7**:517

flowers, growing **5**:348, 349

fly-by-wire technology **1**:29

flying boats **8**:626

flying buttresses **2**:109

flywheels **9**:683

focal length **7**:536

food
  additives **4**:293
  genetically modified **4**:315

food poisoning **4**:294

food preservation **4**:288–289
  fish and shellfish **4**:281

food processors **5**:352, 353

food technology **2**:90; **4**:290–294
  see also baking industry; beverages; brewing; food preservation

footwear
  manufacture **4**:295
  sports shoes **9**:680
  see also leather

forces, and movement **6**:431–432

Ford, Henry **1**:55, 56, 58; **10**:789

Ford, Model T **1**:56; **10**:789

forensic science **4**:296–298

forestry **4**:299–301

forging **6**:447–448

Formula One cars **8**:576

formwork **2**:109

FORTRAN **9**:652

Fortress America **9**:693

fossil fuels **2**:153; **4**:245, 246, 303, 305; **9**:655
  and global warming **8**:568
  and pollution **7**:548
  see also coal; oil and natural gas; peat

foundations **4**:302

foundries, in the United States **2**:123

Fourdrinier, Henry and Sealy **7**:523

fourdriniers **7**:523, 524

Francis turbines **10**:759, 776

Franklin, Benjamin **4**:276

freeways **8**:605

freeze-drying **4**:289

freezers **8**:596

freezing, food **4**:289

Frisch, Otto **7**:499

frit **5**:325

fruit
  growing **5**:348–349
  harvesting **5**:333
  processing **4**:288–289

fruit juices **1**:75

fuel cells **1**:71

fuel injection systems **4**:251

fuels and propellants **4**:273, 303–305

fulcrums **6**:432

Fulton, Robert **9**:686, 713

furnaces **5**:379
  blast **2**:91–92; **5**:379, 381–382
  solar **9**:656

fusion, nuclear **4**:247; **7**:498, 499

Gabor, Dennis **5**:345

Gagarin, Yuri **8**:613; **9**:675

Galilei, Galileo **6**:407; **10**:742

In a modern lithographic press, the image in ink transfers first to the blanket roller and then to the paper.

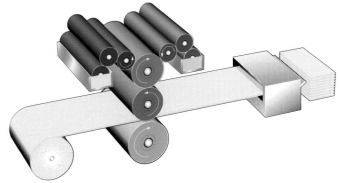

Galileo (space probe) **9**:*668*
Galvani, Luigi **3**:224–225
gamma rays **7**:497; **8**:581
    for sterilization **1**:47
    telescopes **10**:730
Gance, Abel **6**:475–476
gantries **3**:183
garbage disposal **10**:772
Garnerin, André-Jacques **7**:*525*
gas, natural *see* oil and natural gas
gas industry **4**:**306–308**
gasoline **2**:155; **4**:304, **309**
    production **7**:510–511, 513
gastroscopes **3**:238
gas turbines and engines **4**:**310–311**; **6**:422
    helicopter **5**:344
Gatling, Richard Jordan **4**:274
Gatling guns **4**:274
Géant, Le (balloon) **1**:66
gears **4**:**312–313**; **6**:433
    bicycle **1**:76–77, *78*; **6**:430
    in clocks **10**:744
Geiger counters **8**:581
Gemini spacecraft **9**:*679*
generators, electric **3**:219, 222; **6**:420
Genesis (space probe) **9**:*669*
gene therapy **2**:121
genetic engineering **1**:36; **2**:89; **4**:**314–316**; **7**:529
    see also cloning
geophones **7**:505
geothermal energy **4**:**317–318**; **5**:341
Gesner, Abraham **7**:500
geysers **4**:317, 318
Gibbon, John H. **5**:336
Giffard, Henri **1**:30, 67
GIF format **3**:177
gigabytes **9**:688
Gilbert, William **6**:418
gin **1**:75
Giotto (space probe) **9**:*669*

Gladiator (film) **1**: 41; **6**:478
glass, foam **2**:*130*
glass and glassmaking **5**:**324–326**; **9**:*711*
    etching **1**:13
    for optical fibers **4**:267; **5**:326
    recycling **10**:773
Glenn, John **9**:675
gliders **5**:**327**
Global Maritime Distress and Safety System (GMDSS) **6**:424
Global Positioning System (GPS) **1**:57; **5**:**328–329**; **7**:495; **8**:625; **10**:752
    fishing and **4**:279
    for surveys **9**:709
global warming **2**:154; **4**:245, *246–247*, 305; **7**:549; **8**:568
glues **4**:262–263; **10**:798
Glushko, Valentin **8**:614
gluten **1**:64
glycophosphates **7**:528
Goddard, Robert **6**:466; **8**:*612*–613
gold **6**:444
    finding **6**:461
Goodyear, Charles **8**:617
Google (search engine) **5**:*374*
Gould, Gordon **5**:390
graders **3**:179
grafting, plants **5**:351
grain
    elevators **4**:*261*
    harvesting **5**:333
    storage **4**:261
Grand Coulee Dam **5**:359
graphical user interfaces (GUIs) **3**:177; **9**:653
gravimeters **6**:461

gravimetric exploration **7**:505–506
gravity, acceleration due to **6**:431
gravure **8**:574
Great Britain (ship) **2**:144; **8**:636
Great Eastern (ship) **2**:144; **8**:636
Great Exhibition (1851) **2**:110–111
Greathead, James Henry **9**:698
Great Pyramid of Khufu **2**:110
Great Wall of China **2**:*142*
greenhouse effect **7**:549
    see also global warming
grenades **2**:95
grids, power **3**:215
    see also cable, electrical
Griffith, D. W. **6**:475
Groening, Matt **1**:40, 41
Gropius, Walter **3**:201
Grumman Flagstaff (gunboat) **5**:361
GT racing **8**:577
GUIs (graphical user interfaces) **3**:177; **9**:653
gum arabic **1**:16
gunboats, hydrofoil **5**:361
guncotton (nitrocellulose) **4**:270
gunpowder **4**:257; **8**:610
    firearms **4**:272, 273
    forensic science and **4**:297
guns *see* firearms
Gunter's chain **9**:707
Gurney, Goldsworthy **9**:686–687
Gutenberg, Johannes **8**:570, *571*

gypsum **2**:127
gyroscopes **6**:470; **7**:494, 495

Haber (Haber-Bosch) process **2**:125, 140; **4**:265
Hahn, Otto **7**:499
hair, forensic science and **4**:298
hair driers **5**:353
Hale, William **8**:611
Hall, Robert **5**:390
Hall-Héroult process **3**:225
HALO and HAHO techniques **7**:525
hand tools **5**:**330–331**
hardness, Mohs' scale of **1**:13
Harpoon missiles **6**:467
harps **7**:488
Harrier jump jets **1**:25
Harrison, John **5**:328; **7**:*493*, 494–495
harrows (cultivators) **3**:184
harvesting machinery **5**:**332–333**
Harvey, William **9**:704
Hawking, Stephen **10**:*769*
Hawk missiles **6**:467–468
hay **4**:261
hay fever **5**:*365*
hazardous waste **5**:334
headlights, ultraviolet **2**:113
hearing **1**:14
heart, electrocardiograms (ECGs) **6**:439–440
heart attacks, chaos theory and **2**:132
heart disease **7**:534
heart-lung machines **5**:**335–336**
heat exchangers **1**:23; **5**:337, 341
heating systems **5**:**338–341**
    see also air conditioning
heat pumps **5**:341
HEAT shells **2**:95
heat sinks **5**:337

Volume numbers are in **boldface type** followed by colons. Page numbers in **boldface type** refer to main articles and their illustrations; page numbers in *italic type* refer to picture captions.

helicopters **5**:342–344
  see also flight
heliostats **9**:656
helium, uses **4**:308
hematite **2**:91; **5**:378
Henry, Joseph **10**:793
heparin **5**:336
heptane **4**:309
herbicides *see* pesticides and
    herbicides
Hercules aircraft **1**:*28*
Hertz, Heinrich **8**:583;
    10:734, 793–794
highways *see* roads
Hindenburg (airship) **1**:67
hips, artificial **2**:86–87
Hiroshima **7**:*500*
histamine **5**:366
HIV **5**:366
Hoe, Richard March **8**:570
holography **5**:345–347, 391
holovideo **5**:347
Hong Kong
    airport **1**:*32*
    Bionic Tower **9**:647
    Cross-Harbor Tunnel
        10:757
Hooke, Robert **6**:459;
    10:744
Hoover, William **10**:760
Hoover Dam **3**:*190*, 191
hoppers **3**:184
hormone replacement
    therapy (HRT) **7**:534
hormones
    drugs based on **7**:534
    plant **1**:20; **5**:351
horses **1**:*38*
    fitness **10**:765
    tack and horseshoes **1**:38
horticulture **5**:348–351
    see also cloning
hot dry rock technology
    4:318
household appliances
    5:352–353
    electric razors **5**:353
    electric toothbrushes
        5:353

food processors **5**:*352*,
    353
hair driers **5**:353
irons **5**:352–353
sewing machines **2**:151,
    152; **5**:353
stoves and ovens **5**:339,
    353; **9**:690–691
vacuum cleaners **5**:353;
    10:760
washing machines and
    dishwashers
    10:770–771
hovercraft **5**:354–355
    military **5**:354
Howard, Albert **7**:518
Howe, Elias **5**:353
HPVs (human-powered
    vehicles) **1**:78
HST (Hubble Space
    Telescope) **8**:625;
    9:*665*; **10**:729
HTML (Hypertext Mark-
    up Language) **5**:374;
    7:485; **9**:653
HTTP (HyperText
    Transfer Protocol)
    5:374
Hubble Space Telescope
    (HST) **8**:625; **9**:*665*;
    10:729
hulls **8**:564, 635
    displacement **8**:565
    longship **8**:620–621
    testing **8**:619
Human Genome Project
    4:316
human-powered vehicles
    (HPVs) **1**:78
humans, cloning **2**:149
humidity, measuring **6**:431
hurricanes **8**:*622*
Hussey, Obed **9**:713
Huygens, Christiaan **8**:582;
    9:685; **10**:743, 783
hybridization **5**:350
hybrid vehicles **3**:223
hydrants, fire **4**:276
hydraulics **5**:356–357

brake systems **2**:96–*97*;
    5:*357*
excavators **3**:178; **5**:356
for robotic arms
    8:608–609
shock absorbers **1**:63
tractor systems **10**:752
hydrocarbons **2**:138
    from crude oil **7**:511,
        512–513
hydrodesulfurization **7**:513
hydroelectricity **2**:*145*;
    3:216; **4**:247;
    5:358–359; **10**:776,
    781
    turbines **5**:358, *359*;
        8:*566*; **10**:*758–759*
hydrofoils **5**:360–361
    military **5**:361
hydrogen, isotopes **7**:501
hydrogenation **2**:125
hydroponics **5**:350
hygrometers **6**:451
hyperopia **6**:407
Hypertext Mark-up
    Language (HTML)
    5:374; **7**:485; **9**:653
HyperText Transfer
    Protocol (HTTP)
    5:374
hypnotic drugs **7**:534
hypocausts **5**:*340*

ICBMs (intercontinental
    ballistic missiles)
    8:613–614, 615
    see also strategic defense
        systems
icebreakers **9**:650
icons, computer **3**:177
ICUs (intensive care units)
    5:371; **6**:443
ignition systems **1**:57;
    5:362–363
image compression **3**:207

imaging
    medical *see* medical
        imaging
    multispectral **8**:624
immunology **5**:364–366
impedance **3**:217
inbreeding **1**:36
Incas **9**:712
inches **6**:425
incinerators **10**:773
inclinometers **6**:420
Indianapolis 500 (Indy 500)
    8:577
induction, electrostatic
    3:213
inductors **3**:217, *218*, 231
Industrial Revolution **2**:91;
    4:304; **5**:379–380;
    6:464; **7**:548;
    9:712–713
    water power **10**:776
inertia **6**:432
influenza **1**:45
information theory **5**:367
infrared radiation,
    telescopes **10**:730
injections, drug **7**:530

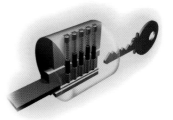

*The right key raises pin
tumblers in a Yale lock
to open the lock.*

inks 3:165; 4:298
  printing 8:571
insecticides *see* pesticides
    and herbicides
insects, and forensic science
    4:297, *298*
insemination, artificial
    6:412
instruments, musical *see*
    musical instruments
insulation 5:368
  acoustic 5:368
  electrical 3:213; 5:368
  thermal 5:368
insulin 6:439; 7:534
  biotechnology and 2:*89,
    90*; 4:316
integrated circuits (silicon
    chips; microchips)
    3:172, *174, 231, 232*;
    5:369–370; 8:633
  manufacture 3:232;
    5:369–*370*
  PLCs 3:228
integrated pest
    management (IPM)
    3:187; 7:529
integrated services digital
    network *see* ISDN
intensive care units (ICUs)
    5:371; 6:443
intercom systems 6:455
interference 10:783
interferons 2:121
International Space Station
    4:*252*; 8:625;
    9:*672–673*
Internet 3:175; 5:372–374;
    7:485
  and the MP3 controversy
    9:660
  radio 8:584
  retailing on 8:598
  security 8:630
  television 10:732
Internet Protocol (IP)
    numbers 5:372
Internet Service Providers
    (ISPs) 5:372, 374

Interstate Highway System,
    U.S. 8:603
intranets 5:373
inventions 5:375–377;
    9:713
  see also technology, history
    of
iodine, antiseptics based on
    1:46
ions 3:212; 8:580
  positive and negative
    7:497
Iron Age 9:711
irons 5:352–353
iron and steel 5:330,
    378–383; 6:446
  bridges 2:102–103;
    5:*383*
  building with 2:110–111;
    5:*378*; 9:646, 647
  cast iron 5:379
  production 2:*91–92*;
    4:308; 5:378–383;
    6:*445, 449*; 9:*713*
  rusting 3:182
  steel 2:94; 5:379–*383*;
    6:*445, 448, 449*
  wrought iron 5:378
  see also blast furnace;
    mining
irradiation, food 4:289;
    7:497
irrigation 5:384–387;
    10:778
  chemigation 3:187
ISDN (integrated services
    digital network)
    3:167, 207; 5:373;
    10:726, 727
isobars and isotherms 6:451
isomerization 7:514
isooctane 4:309
isopropyl alcohol 1:46

isotopes 7:496–497
  separation 2:129
Itaipu Dam 2:*145*

Jahre Viking (ship) 7:515,
    552
jamming signals 3:229
Japan, bridges 2:107
Java (programming
    language) 9:653
Jazz Singer, The (film) 6:476
jeeps, U.S. Army 7:502
Jenner, Edward 5:*366*
jetfoils 5:*361*
jetties 7:553
joints (body), replacement
    2:86–87
joints (mechanical) 4:262
Jones, Brian 1:67
JPEG format 3:177
junks 8:621
Jupiter, space probes to
    9:*668–669*

Kaiser, Henry 8:635
karting 8:576–577
keels 8:621
Kelly, William 5:379
Kelvin temperature scale
    10:741–742
Kennedy Space Center
    5:392, *394*
Kepler (space probe) 9:667
kerogen 7:504
kerosene 4:304; 6:410;
    7:510
Kettering, Charles 6:466
kettledrums 7:489
Kevlar 4:268, *269, 271*
keyboards, electronic 7:*489*
Khufu, Great Pyramid of
    2:110
kieselgurh 4:258

Kilby, Jack 5:370
kilns 2:100
kilobytes 9:688
kilowatt-hours 3:218
kinetoscopes 6:474
Kittinger, Joseph 1:67
knitting 10:739
knocking 4:251, 309; 5:363
knots (speed) 7:495
Koenig, Friedrich 8:570
Korolyov, Sergey 8:614
krypton 4:308
Kurzweil, Raymond 10:769

Lacquer 7:521
lactic acid 3:189
ladybugs 2:84
Laerdal Tunnel 10:757
lager 2:99
laminar flow 1:17
La Mountain, John 1:66
lamps
  arc 6:411
  fluorescent 6:411
  oil 6:410
  see also lightbulbs
landfills 5:334; 7:549;
    10:772
Landsat satellites 9:709
landscaping, hard
    3:178–179
Landsteiner, Karl 2:93
languages, multimedia
    7:485
LANs (local area networks)
    3:167
Lanston, Tolbert 8:570
laser disks 10:767
lasers 5:388–391; 6:411
  CD players 3:168, 169;
    5:390–391
  cutting 2:151; 5:*389*, 390;
    6:411
  fiber optics 9:716
  space 9:693
  surgery using 5:390–391;
    9:*705*
  to record race winners
    9:681

Volume numbers are in **boldface type** followed
by colons. Page numbers in **boldface type** refer to
main articles and their illustrations; page numbers in
italic type refer to picture captions.

used in dentistry **3**:199

used in holography **5**:*345, 346*–347, 391

used in surveying **9**:708–709; **10**:757

weapon-guiding **2**:94, 95; **5**:391

lasing medium **5**:389

lateens **8**:621

lathes **6**:416

latitude **7**:492, 493

launch sites **5**:392–394

launch vehicles **5**:395–397; **9**:662

Laval, Carl de **2**:128

Lavoisier, Antoine **2**:139, 140

LCDs *see* liquid-crystal displays

lead **6**:446

leather **5**:**398**

leatherette **5**:398

Leclanché, Georges **1**:70

LEDs (light-emitting diodes) **3**:231; **4**:267

Leeuwenhoek, Antonie van **6**:459

legs, artificial **2**:87

legumes **3**:185

Lenard, Philipp **6**:436

Lenormand, Louis-Sebastien **7**:525

lenses **6**:405–406, *407*

camera **7**:536–537, *540*

in microscopes **6**:456

Leonardo da Vinci **5**:377; **7**:525

Lesseps, Ferdinand de **2**:116, 118

letterpress **8**:571–572

levees **3**:191

levers **6**:*432*, 433

Liberty ships **8**:635

lice, head **6**:*459*

lift **4**:*282, 283*

ligands **7**:532

light and optics **6**:**404–407**

and color **3**:164

fiber optics **3**:*167;*

4:**266–267**; **5**:*326,* 391; **6**:406

laser light *see* lasers

light particles **5**:389; **6**:404

light waves **5**:346, 389; **6**:404

monochromatic light **5**:389

photoelectric cells **3**:233; **4**:260

speed of light **6**:406–407

telescopes **10**:728, *730*

ultraviolet light **3**:*164;* **6**:*411*

lightbulbs **3**:*230;* **6**:*411*

see also lamps

lighthouses **6**:**408–409**

construction **6**:409

lighting **6**:**410–411**

electric **6**:*410*–411; **9**:712

gas **6**:410; **9**:712

oil **6**:410

lights

brake **3**:201

see also lamps; lightbulbs; lighting

lightships **6**:409

lignite (brown coal) **2**:153, *154;* **4**:304

limbs, artificial **2**:87

limestone, for cement **2**:101, *126,* 127

Lindstrand, Per **1**:67

linear accelerators **2**:*120*

liners **8**:638

Linotype **8**:570

liquefied natural gas (LNG) **4**:307

liquefied petroleum gas (LPG) **4**:304, 307

liquid-crystal displays (LCDs) **3**:*206;* **10**:733–734

watches with **10**:745

Lister, Joseph **1**:46; **9**:704

lithography **8**:*572–573*

livestock farming **1**:21; **6**:**412–413**

cloning and **2**:149

veterinary medicine and **10**:*763,* 764

llamas **1**:37

loaders **3**:180

lobsters, fishing for **4**:281

local area networks (LANs) **3**:167

Lockerbie bombing **8**:629

locks, canal **2**:116–117, *119*

locks and safes **6**:**414–415**; **8**:628

Locomotion (locomotive) **8**:587

lodestones **6**:418

LOES (Low Orbiting Earth Satellites) **3**:167

Loewy, Raymond **3**:201

logic gates **3**:172; **7**:491

longitude **5**:328; **7**:492, *493,* 494–495

Long March rockets **5**:*395,* 397

longships **8**:620–621

looms **10**:*738,* 739, *740*

Lorenz, Edward **2**:132

lost wax process (casting) **2**:123

loudspeakers **6**:*455;* **9**:658; **10**:725

see also microphones

Lovelace, Ada, Countess of **9**:652

low Earth orbits (LEOs) **8**:624

Lowell, Francis Cabot **10**:738

LPG (liquefied petroleum gas) **4**:304, 307

Lucite **7**:544

luges **9**:649

Lumière, Auguste and Louis **6**:474

Lunar Orbiter space probes **9**:666

Lunar Prospector (space probe) **9**:666

Luna space probes **9**:666

Lunik space probes **9**:665–666

lute family **7**:488–489

lymphocytes **5**:365

lyres **7**:488

M cCormick, Cyrus **6**:428; **9**:713

machine guns **4**:*274*

machine tools **6**:**416–417**

Macintosh, Charles **8**:616

mad cow disease (BSE) **6**:412; **10**:765

magazines, gun **4**:274

Magellan (space probe) **9**:666, 667

In a pneumatic gate valve, the booster fan increases air pressure behind the capsule to open the valve.

maglevs (magnetic levitation systems) **6**:*418*, 419, 470

magnetic resonance imaging (MRI) **3**:*204*; **6**:*420*, *435–436*, 439

magnetism *see* magnets

magnetite **2**:91; **5**:378

magnetometers **1**:50

magnetometric exploration **4**:306

magnetrons **8**:578; **9**:691

magnets and magnetism **6**:**418–420**

in motors **3**:*220–221*

Maiman, Theodore **5**:390

manga films **1**:40

MANs (metropolitan area networks) **3**:167

mantles, gas **6**:410

manure **4**:*264*, 265

mapmaking **8**:624; **9**:*709*

Marconi, Guglielmo **8**:583; **9**:713, 716; **10**:734–735, *793*, 794, 795

marine engineering **6**:**421–423**

Mariner space probes **9**:666, 667, 668

maritime communication **6**:**424**

markets **8**:597–598

marquetry **10**:797, *798*

Mars

robotic explorers on **8**:*609*

space probes to **9**:667–668, 669

Mars Global Surveyor (space probe) **3**:*167*; **9**:667

marshaling yards **8**:*593*, 594

Marsh, Sylvester **2**:157

Mars Odyssey (space probe) **9**:669

Mars Pathfinder (space probe) **9**:667–668

Martin, Pierre-Emile **5**:381

masers **5**:390

masonry *see* bricks and masonry

mass

and radiation **7**:497–498

and weight **10**:786

matchlocks **4**:272

Mauretania (ship) **9**:687

mauveine **2**:138; **3**:210

Maxim, Hiram **4**:274

Maxwell, James Clerk **8**:582–583

Mayo brothers **9**:703

measurement **6**:**425**

see also weights and measures

meat, processing **4**:290

mechanical advantage **6**:*433*

mechanical engineering **4**:254; **6**:**426–428**

mechanical transmission **6**:**429–430**

automobiles **1**:57; **4**:*313*; **5**:357; **6**:*429–430*

motorcycles **6**:472

mechanics **6**:**431–433**

mechatronics **6**:427

medical imaging **6**:**434–437**, 439

dentistry **3**:198

endoscopy **3**:238; **6**:437

see also diagnostic equipment

medical technology **6**:**438–443**

see also heart-lung machines; medical imaging

megabytes **9**:688

Meitner, Lise **7**:499

melamines **7**:543

Méliès, Georges **1**:39; **6**:475

Mercury

space probes to **9**:667, 668

Mergenthaler, Ottmar **8**:570

meridian, prime **7**:492

Mesopotamians **9**:710; **10**:788

metals **6**:**444–449**

alloys **1**:34

casting **2**:*122–123*

corrosion **3**:182

fatigue **6**:444

joining **4**:263

refining **7**:517

transition **2**:124; **6**:446

see also blast furnace; iron and steel; ore extraction

meteorological instruments **6**:**450–451**

meters (units of measurement) **6**:425

methane **2**:138, *139*

methanol **4**:307

metropolitan area networks (MANs) **3**:167

mice, computer **3**:*172*

microbots **8**:609

microchips *see* integrated circuits

micromachines **2**:90; **6**:*452*

see also nanotechnology

micrometeors **9**:*663*

micrometers **5**:*330*, 331

microorganisms

sources of antibiotics **1**:44

see also bacteria

microphones and loudspeakers **3**:227, *228*; **6**:**453–455**; **9**:657–658, *661*; **10**:725, 753

microprinting **1**:69

microprocessors **3**:172; **5**:370; **8**:633

see also integrated circuits

microscopy **6**:406, 438, 439, **456–459**

miles **6**:425

milk **3**:188–*189*

milling **1**:64

mines (explosives) **6**:420; **9**:696

minidiscs **9**:689

mining **6**:**460–465**

coal **2**:*153*; **6**:*464*, 465

deep (underground mines) **2**:153; **6**:462, 465

robotic explorers used in **8**:609

strip (surface mining) **2**:153; **6**:462, 465

Mir (space station) **8**:625; **9**:*670*, 671, 672

Mir I and *II* (submersibles) **3**:195

mirrors **6**:*406*

MIRVs **6**:469

missiles **6**:428, **466–469**; **8**:613–614

missile-detecting radar **9**:693

National Missile Defense (NMD) program **2**:139

see also torpedoes and depth charges

modems **5**:373

see also computers

modular manufacturing **2**:152

Mohs' scale of hardness **1**:13

molding

injection-molding **4**:295; **7**:*546*

plastics **7**:*545*, 546

money **1**:*68–69*

monomers **2**:138

monomobiles **6**:470

monorails **6**:**470**

see also cog railroad

Monotype **8**:570

Montgolfier, Joseph and Jacques **1**:66

Volume numbers are in **boldface type** followed by colons. Page numbers in **boldface type** refer to main articles and their illustrations; page numbers in *italic type* refer to picture captions.

Moon
   landings **5**:*377*; **9**:675–676
   space probes to **9**:665–666
moorings, tanker **7**:513
mopeds **6**:471
morphine **7**:532–533
Morse, Samuel **1**:69; **9**:714, 715; **10**:724
Morse code **8**:583; **9**:*714*, 715; **10**:724
mortar **2**:101, 109, 110
mortars (explosives) **10**:747
moths, gypsy **2**:84
motion
   linear **6**:431
   Newton's laws of **4**:311; **6**:431–432
motorcycles **6**:471–472
motors
   electric *see* electric motors
   outboard and inboard **6**:422
moviemaking **6**:473–478
   see also animation
MP3 format and players **3**:207; **9**:660
MPEGs **10**:768
MRI scans **3**:*204*
mulching **7**:519
mules **1**:38
multimedia **3**:175; **7**:484–485
multiple reentry vehicle (MRV) missiles **6**:469
Murnau, E.W. **6**:475
Mushet, Robert **5**:380
musical instruments **1**:15; **7**:486–489; **10**:*761*
mustard gas **2**:133
myopia **6**:407

Nails **4**:*262*
nanocomputers **7**:491
nanotechnology **7**:490–491
   see also micromachines
naphthenes **7**:511
National Missile Defense (NMD) program **2**:139

Natta, Giulio **7**:511
natural gas *see* oil and natural gas
natural language processing **1**:54
Nautilus, USS (submarine) **6**:423; **9**:695
navigation **7**:492–495
   and the Global Positioning System **5**:328–329; **7**:495
   see also maritime communication
NEAR Shoemaker (space probe) **9**:667, 669
nematicides **7**:528
neon **4**:308
neoprene **4**:268, 270; **8**:617
NERVA rockets **8**:615
nerve gases **2**:133
neuroma, acoustic **6**:436
neutrons **3**:212; **7**:496
Newcomen, Thomas **6**:427; **9**:685–686
newspapers, printing **8**:573
Newton, Isaac **4**:311; **6**:432
nickelodeons **6**:474
nicotine **7**:527
Nipkow, Paul **10**:735, *736*
Nipkow disks **10**:735, *736*
NIST-F1 (clock) **10**:*745*
nitric acid **2**:141
nitrocellulose (guncotton) **4**:270
nitrogen
   in the soil **3**:185; **4**:264
   liquid **4**:308
   uses **4**:307–308
nitroglycerin **4**:258, 273
Nobel, Alfred **4**:258
noble gases **4**:308
noise **3**:233
North Star **7**:493
Noyce, Robert **5**:370
nuclear energy **4**:*244*, 247; **7**:496–499
   nuclear-powered engines **6**:422–423
   nuclear submarines **6**:*421*,

423; **7**:499; **9**:696, *697*
   see also nuclear weapons
nuclear quadrupole resonance **1**:50
nuclear weapons **7**:500–501
   atomic bombs **7**:498, 500–501
   thermonuclear (hydrogen bombs) **7**:499, 501
nylon **4**:270, 271
   for fishing nets **4**:279

Oberth, Hermann **8**:613
oboes **7**:488
oceans
   thermal energy from **10**:777
   wave power **10**:784–785
off-road vehicles **7**:502–503
Ohain, Hans von **6**:428
O'Hare International Airport (Chicago) **1**:*31*, 32
oil and natural gas **4**:245, 304; **7**:504–509
   limited supplies **4**:246
   natural gas **4**:*306–307*
   oil refining **4**:308; **7**:510–515
   oil spills **7**:515, 550, 551
oil(s)
   automobile engine **1**:58
   processing **4**:291–292
oil shale **7**:509
oil wells **7**:506–507

Olds, Ransom Eli **1**:55
Olmecs **9**:712
open-hearth process **5**:381, *382*
operating rooms **9**:*703*, 705–706
opiates **7**:533
optics *see* light and optics
ore extraction **7**:516–517
organic farming **7**:518–519
organophosphates **7**:528
organs (musical instruments) **7**:489
Orlon **4**:271
Orsted, Hans Christian **6**:419
oscillating water columns (OWCs) **10**:785
Otis, Elisha Graves **2**:111; **3**:237; **9**:646
outbreeding **1**:36
ovens *see* stoves and ovens
oxides **7**:516
oxygen, uses **4**:308
oysters **1**:49
ozone layer, reduction **4**:308

Pacemakers, heart **2**:87
pack animals **1**:37

When all the forces operating on an automobile at rest on a slope balance, the vehicle remains stationary.

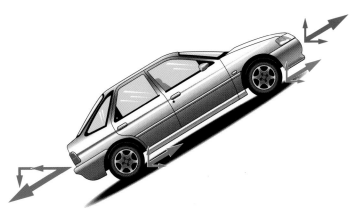

paddle steamers **6**:422

paddy fields **5**:384, *387*

pagers **10**:726

painkillers **7**:532–533

paints and surface coatings **7:520–521**

mixing **3**:*165*

palmtops *see* personal digital assistants

Panama Canal **2**:116, 118

Pan-American Highway **8**:605

panthenol **2**:147

paper and papermaking **7:522–524**

recycling **7**:524; **10**:773

Papin, Denis **9**:685

parabolic trough solar collectors **9**:656

parachutes **7:525**

parasitoids **2**:84–85

Park, Nick **1**:40

Parsons, Charles **9**:687

particle accelerators **6**:420

particleboard **10**:797

Pasteur, Louis **1**:44; **6**:438

pasteurization **3**:189; **4**:288

pathenogenesis **2**:149

Patriot missiles **6**:468

PCBs (polychlorinated biphenyls) **7**:550

PCR (polymerase chain reaction) **3**:205

pearls **1**:49

peat **2**:153; **4**:245, *304*

Pelton wheels **10**:758–*759*, 776

penicillin **1**:*44*, 45

Penicillium **1**:*44*, 45

percussion instruments **7**:487, 489

Perkin, William **2**:138; **3**:210

Persian wheels **5**:386

personal digital assistants (PDAs; palmtops) **3**:175; **7:526**; **9**:*689*

see also micromachines; nanocomputers

pest control **1**:20–21

biological control **2:84–85**

see also pesticides and herbicides

pesticides and herbicides **1**:21; **3**:185, 186–187; **7:527–529**

pollution from **7**:529, 550–551

PET (polyester terephthalate) **7**:545

petroleum (crude oil) *see* oil and natural gas

phagocytes **5**:364

pharmaceuticals **7**:530

industry **7**:533

pharmacology **7:530–534**

see also antibiotics; medical technology

pharmacopoeias **7**:532

phenol **1**:46

phenylalanine **2**:*139*

pheromones **3**:187

phonographs **9**:657, 658–659

phosphorus, in fertilizers **4**:265

photocells (photoelectric cells) **3**:233; **4**:259–260

photoconductive cells **4**:260

photoemissive cells **4**:*259*, 260

photovoltaic cells **4**:260; **9**:655

photocopiers **7:535**

photodiodes **4**:267

photoelectric cells *see* photocells

photography **7:536–541**

aerial **1**:50; **7**:541

color sensitivity and balance **7**:539–540

developing film **7**:540–541

digital **3**:207; **7**:*537*

exposure **7**:538

film **7**:537–538, 539–541

filters **7**:540

flashes **7**:540

photolamps **7**:540

producing prints **7**:541

shutter speed **7**:538–539

photolamps **7**:540

photomasking **3**:*230*, 232

photons **5**:389; **6**:404

photosynthesis **4**:245

phthalocyanines **7**:520

physics, particle **8**:581

physiology **9**:703–704

pianos **7**:*488*, 489

Piccard, Bertrand **1**:67

pickle-fork boats **8**:565

pickups **10**:755

piers **7**:553

piezoelectric effect **6**:455

pigments **3**:165

pigs **6**:413

pile drivers **4**:302

piles **4**:302

pilots, harbor **7**:552

Pioneer space probes **9**:666, 668

pipelines

bulk materials **10**:762

oil **7**:514, 515

water **10**:781

pitch (torque) **4**:*282*, 285

Pitman arms **1**:60–61

pivots **4**:262

pixels

CCD **10**:766

computer graphics **3**:176–177

fax machines **4**:260

plague **10**:765

planes (hand tools) **5**:*330*, 331; **10**:*797*, 798

planes, inclined, on canals **2**:117–118

planing **8**:564

planing machines **6**:417

planting, companion **7**:519, 527

plants

cells **2**:89

cloning **2**:148

grafting **5**:351

grown from seeds **5**:350

hormones **1**:20; **5**:351

transgenic **4**:*316*

see also crop farming; crops; forestry; horticulture; trees

plasma, blood **2**:93

plastics **2**:138; **7:542–546**

aircraft construction **1**:28

casting **2**:123

molding **7**:*545*, 546

recycling **7**:546; **10**:773

platelets **2**:93; **5**:364

platinum **6**:446

PLCs (programmable logic chips) **3**:228

Plexiglas **7**:544, 546

plowing **3**:184

contour **1**:20

see also crop farming; tractors

plows **7:547**

plutonium, and atomic bombs **7**:500

plywood **10**:797

PMMA (polymethyl methacrylate **7**:544

pneumatics **5**:357

for robotic arms **8**:609

point of sale **8**:598

Polaris **7**:493

polders **2**:143

polishes **7**:521

pollarding **4**:299–300

Volume numbers are in **boldface type** followed by colons. Page numbers in **boldface type** refer to main articles and their illustrations; page numbers in *italic type* refer to picture captions.

pollen, allergies to **5**:*365*
pollination **5**:349–350
pollution **7**:**548–551**
  air **4**:246; **7**:548–550
  bacteria and **2**:90; **7**:551
  by pesticides **7**:529,
    550–551
  hazardous waste **5**:334
  landfills **5**:334; **7**:549;
    10:772
  oil spills **7**:515, 550, 551
  waste treatment
    10:**772–775**
  water **2**:*147*; **7**:550–551
  see also cleaning agents;
    global warming;
    recycling
polychlorinated biphenyls
  (PCBs) **7**:550
polyester **4**:271; **10**:738
polyester terephthalate
  (PET) **7**:545
polyethylene **2**:86, 125,
  138; **7**:511, 542, 543
  manufacture **7**:545
polymerase chain reaction
  (PCR) **3**:205; **4**:297
polymerases **4**:314
polymers **2**:125, 138; **4**:271;
  7:511, 543
  condensation **7**:545
polymethyl methacrylate
  (PMMA) **7**:544
polypropylene **7**:511, 542,
  543
polystyrene **7**:543
polytetrafluoroethylene
  (PTFE; Teflon) **7**:544
polyvinyl chloride (PVC)
  2:140; **7**:542, 544;
  10:740
Pompidou Center, Paris
  4:*253*
pontoon boats **8**:565
porcelain **7**:557, *558*
ports **2**:143; **7**:**552–555**
  naval **7**:*552*, 555
  see also maritime
    communication

positron emission
    tomography (PET)
    6:437, 439
potassium **6**:444–445
  in fertilizers **4**:265
potassium hydroxide
    (caustic potash) **2**:141
potential difference **3**:214
pottery **7**:**556–558**
  see also ceramics
Poulsen, Valdemar **10**:794
poultry **6**:413
pounds (units of
    measurement) **6**:425
powder coatings **7**:521
powerboats **8**:**564–565**
power lines **3**:*214*
  accessing the Internet via
    3:167
power stations **3**:215–216,
    222; **8**:**566–568**
  burning fossil fuels **5**:358;
    8:566, *567–568*
  gas **4**:304
  geothermal **4**:*318*
  hydroelectric **5**:359–*359*;
    8:566
  IGCC plants **2**:155
  nuclear **4**:*244*, 247;
    7:*498–499*; **8**:566
  oil-fired **8**:567
  solar **4**:252; **9**:656
  thermal **8**:566, 567–568
  use of coal **2**:155; **8**:*567*
  see also electricity
    transmission
power take off shafts
  10:752
pozzolana **2**:111–112
precipitators, electrostatic
  1:22; **8**:567
prime movers **3**:222
printers, desktop **8**:*574*
printing **7**:522–523;
  8:**569–574**
  bank bills **1**:69
  history **8**:570, 571
programmable logic chips
  (PLCs) **3**:228

programming, computer *see*
    software and
    programming
projectors, movie **6**:478
Prontosil Red **1**:44
propellants **4**:305
  firearm **4**:273
propellers, ship **2**:*123*;
    9:**644**
propylene **7**:511
prostheses **2**:87
proteins **2**:139; **4**:292
  fibers made from **4**:269
Proton rockets **5**:397
protons **3**:212; **7**:496
prototypes **4**:252; **6**:425
Prowler (aircraft) **3**:*229*
Prozac **7**:534
PTFE (polytetrafluoro-
    ethylene; Teflon)
    7:544
puddle (construction
    material) **2**:115–116
puddling process **5**:380
pulleys **6**:*433*
pumps **8**:**575**
PVC *see* polyvinyl chloride
pylons, electricity **3**:*215*
pyramids, Egyptian **2**:110;
    9:709
pyrethrum **7**:528
Pythagoras, and music
    7:486

Quadraphonic sound
    9:661
quarantine, animal
    10:764–765
quarrying **6**:462, 463
quartz, in clocks **10**:745
Queen Elizabeth II (ship)
    8:638
Quimby, Harriet **4**:287

Race cars **1**:19;
    8:**576–577**; **10**:746,
    789
racing
  horse **10**:765
  motorcycle **6**:472
rack and pinion **1**:61
radar **8**:**578–579**
  aircraft invisible to *see*
    stealth aircraft
  archeology and **1**:50
  electronic
    countermeasures
    3:229
  fishing and **4**:279
  missile-detecting **9**:*693*
radiation, medical uses
    7:497

A machining center can carry 100 or more different tools in a rotating magazine.

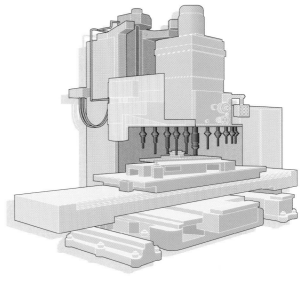

radiation (heat) **5**:338, 339, 368

radiation (ionizing) **7**:497; **8**:580–581

  detection **8:580–581**

radiators, heat exchangers and **5**:337

radio **1**:*43*; **8:582–584**; **9**:716–717; **10**:*793–795*

  amplifiers **1**:35

  cellular and satellite phones using **3**:167; **8**:582; **10**:*726*

  clockwork **5**:*375*

  digital **8**:584; **10**:795

  frequency bands **1**:43; **8**:582; **10**:794

  GPS **5**:329

  Internet **8**:584

  waves **8**:582; **10**:793, 794

  see also radar; television; wireless communication

radioactivity **7:496–497**

radioactive waste **5**:*334*

radiocarbon dating **1**:51; **7**:497

radiography, digital **3**:198

radioisotopes **3**:205; **7**:497

radiosondes **6**:451

radiotagging **8**:*583*; **10**:*794*

radio telescopes **10**:729–730

radiotherapy **2**:*120*, 121

radon **8**:581

rafts, Cockerell's **10**:785

railroad cars **8:585–588**

railroads

  cable-operated **2**:158

  cog **2:157–158**

  construction **8:589–591**

  gauge **8**:585

  light railroads **8**:587

  operation **8:592–594**

  points **3**:228; **8**:*594*

  signals **8**:*592–593*, 594

  U.S. mileage **8**:589

  see also railroad cars;

subway systems; trains; tunnels

rain, acid **2**:154; **7**:*549, 550*; **8**:567

Rainbow (ship) **8**:636

rain gauges **6**:*450*, 451

raising machines **10**:740

ramps **6**:433

Rance barrage **10**:777

Ranger space probes **9**:666

rarefaction **10**:782

rasps **10**:798

rayon **4**:270

razors, electric **5**:353

RDX **4**:258

reactors **2**:134, 135–136

reaping machines **9**:713

records (vinyl discs) **9**:*658, 659*

recycling **10**:773

  glass **10**:773

  metals **6**:447; **10**:773

  paper **7**:524; **10**:773

  plastics **7**:546; **10**:773

  waste treatment **10:772–775**

  see also hazardous waste

reduction **5**:378

reed beds **2**:145

reefers **10**:755

refining, metals **7**:517

reflection **6**:*404–405, 406*

  total internal **4**:266; **6**:406

refraction **6**:405

refractive index **4**:266, 267

refrigeration **8:595–596**

  and air-conditioning systems **1**:23

  crops **4**:261

  food **4**:288–289

  heat exchangers and **5**:337, 341

registers, cash **8**:598–599

relays **3**:*228*

  reed **3**:227

remotely operated vehicles (ROVs) **3**:195; **10**:749

Remote Manipulator System (RMS) **9**:677

Renaissance **9**:712

rennin **3**:189

repeaters **4**:267

reservoirs **3**:190, 191; **5**:358–359, 384

resistance, electrical **3**:214

resistance meters, electrical **1**:50

resistors **3**:217, 231, *233*

retail industry **8:597–599**

  store security **8**:628, *629*

retina **3**:164; **6**:407

reusable launch vehicles (RLVs) **5**:396

revolvers **4**:*273*, 274

Reynaud, Emile **6**:473

rhinoplasty **9**:706

rice **3**:184; **5**:384, *387*

Richter scale **8**:631

rifling **4**:273

rigs, oil **7**:506, *507–508*

Rittenhouse, William **7**:523

rivets **4**:262

roads **8:600–605**

  and the environment **2**:145

road trains **10**:755

Robert, Nicholas-Louis **7**:523

robotic flight **8:606–607**

robotics **1**:*54*; **8:608–609**; **9**:677

  robotic inspectors **8**:609; **10**:749

  telesurgery **6**:442

Rocket (locomotive) **8**:587

rockets **8:610–615**

launch sites **5:392–394**

launch vehicles **5:395–397**; **9**:662

  Saturn V **5**:392, 393, *396–397*; **8**:*610*

rods and cones **3**:164

see also missiles; space probes

Roebling, John and Washington **2**:106

Roget, Peter **6**:473

roll **4**:*282*, 285

Romans, ancient **9**:711

  cement and concrete **2**:111–112, 126

  civil engineering **2**:142

  firefighting **4**:275

  glass **9**:*711*

Romer, Olaus **6**:407

Röntgen, Wilhelm Konrad **6**:434, 436

rooms

  "clean" **1**:22

  strong **6**:415

routers **5**:372

ROVs *see* remotely operated vehicles

rubber **8:616–617**; **10**:746

rudders

  aircraft **4**:286

  ship **9**:645

rust **3**:182

Rutherford, Ernest **7**:497

S addles **1**:38

Safeguard system **9**:692

safes *see* locks and safes

sailing **8:618–621**

St. Lawrence Seaway **2**:118, 119

Sakigake (space probe) **9**:669

salicin **7**:532

Salmonella **4**:294

Salter's ducks **10**:784–*785*

salting, food **4**:289

Salvarsan **1**:44

Salyut space stations **9**:670–671

Volume numbers are in **boldface type** followed by colons. Page numbers in **boldface type** refer to main articles and their illustrations; page numbers in *italic type* refer to picture captions.

sandblasting **1**:*12*, 13
sandpaper **10**:798
sarin **2**:133
satellites **8**:*622–625*;
    9:*674–675*
  astronomical **8**:624
  communications **3**:*167*;
    8:622–623, *624*, 625;
    10:727
  control systems
    8:622–623
  Global Positioning
    System **5**:*328–329*;
    7:495; **8**:625
  laser-powered
    microsatellites **5**:391
  launch vehicles
    5:*395–397*; **8**:622
  military **8**:624–625;
    9:692–693
  orbits **5**:395; **8**:622, *624*
  power systems **8**:623–624
  remote-sensing **8**:624
  rocket motors **8**:615
  surveying **9**:*709*
  weather **6**:451; **8**:*622*, 624
  see also rockets; space
    probes; space station;
    space travel
Saturn, space probes to
    9:*663, 666, 668, 669*
Saturn V rockets **5**:392,
    393, *396–397*; **8**:*610*,
    615
sawmills **4**:300
saws **5**:331; **10**:798
  power **6**:417
saxophones **7**:487, 488
SBLs (space-based lasers)
    9:693
scaffolding **2**:109
scales, electronic **10**:787
scanners, computer **3**:206
scanning electron
    microscopes (SEMs)
    6:*457*, 458
scanning tunneling
    microscopes (STMs)
    6:459

Schawlow, Arthur **5**:390
Schott, Otto **5**:326
scooters, motor **6**:471
  see also motorcycles
scrapers **3**:179
screws **4**:263
screwworms, biological
    control of **2**:85
scuba diving **3**:*192*, 193
scythes **5**:330, 332, *333*
sealants **7**:521
seaplanes **8**:626
search engines (computing)
    5:*374*
Sea Skua missiles **6**:467
seawater, distillation **10**:779
seaweed **1**:*48*
security equipment
    8:**627–630**
  at airports **1**:33;
    8:628–629, *630*
  see also locks and safes
seeds
  growing plants from
    5:350
  sowing **3**:184
Seikan Tunnel **10**:757
seiners **4**:*279*, 280
seismograms **8**:631
seismographs **8**:631
seismography **6**:461; **7**:505;
    8:**631**
semaphore **6**:424; **8**:592
semiconductors **3**:231–232;
    5:369–370; **8**:583,
    632–633
  in solar cells **9**:656
semitrailers **10**:754, *755*
SEMs (scanning electron
    microscopes) **6**:*457*,
    458
Seneca, Lucius **6**:459
Senefelder, Aloys **8**:570,
    572
Sentinel system **9**:692
September 11 attacks **8**:629
septic tanks **10**:774
servers, computer **9**:*688*
Seto-Ohashi Bridge **2**:107

sewage, treatment
    10:*773–775*
sewing machines **2**:151,
    152; **5**:353
sextants **5**:328; **7**:493
shadufs **5**:384, *386*
shampoos **2**:147
Shannon, Claude Elwood
    5:367
sheep **6**:413
  cloning **2**:*148*, 149
  dipping **1**:*47*
shellfish, aquaculture **1**:49
shells *see* bombs and shells
Shepard, Alan **9**:675
ships and boats **8**:**634–638**
  aircraft carriers **1**:24–25;
    6:423
  building **8**:636–638
  bulk carriers **6**:*423*; **7**:554
  canal boats **2**:119
  cargo **7**:554–555
  container ships **6**:*423*;
    7:554; **8**:*634*
  cruise ships **7**:555
  design **8**:635–636
  drill ships **7**:507
  fastest **8**:564–565
  fishing vessels **4**:278–279,
    280, 281
  hovercraft **5**:**354–355**
  hydrofoils **5**:**360–361**
  icebreakers **9**:650
  launching **8**:637
  measuring speed of **7**:495
  propellers **2**:*123*; **9**:**644**
  rudders **9**:**645**
  sailing **8**:**618–621**
  tankers **2**:*123*; **7**:514–515,
    551
  tug boats **7**:552
  see also maritime
    communication;
    navigation; ports

shock absorbers **1**:62, 63
Shockley, William **3**:230
shoes *see* footwear; leather
shops *see* retail industry
shortsightedness **6**:407
shot **4**:273
shot blasting **1**:13
Shrapnel, Henry **2**:95
sick building syndrome
    1:23
sickles **5**:332, *333*
Sidewinder missiles **6**:467,
    468
Siemens, William **5**:380
sight *see* vision
Sikorsky, Igor **5**:343, *344*
silage **4**:261; **5**:333
silencers **4**:274
Silent Spring (book) **7**:528
silicon carbide
    (carborundum) **1**:12
silicon chips *see* integrated
    circuits
silk **4**:269
silver **6**:446, 447
Simpsons, The (cartoon
    show) **1**:40, 41
S.I. units **6**:425
skates, ice **9**:649
skiboards **9**:649
skiffs **8**:564
ski lifts **2**:158
skis **9**:648–649
Skylab (space station) **9**:*671*
skyscrapers **2**:111; **5**:*378*;
    9:**646–647**

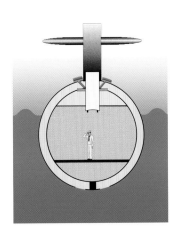

**To allow a submarine to
surface, the diving
planes point upward to
let air fill the tanks.**

slash-and-burn agriculture **4**:300
sleds **1**:37; **9**:*649*
sleighs **9**:*649*
slide bars **4**:262
slopers **2**:150, 151
smallpox **2**:133; **5**:366
Smeaton, John **2**:126–127, 143
smelting **6**:447; **7**:517
smog **7**:548
snails, biological control **2**:85
snowblowers **9**:650
snowcats **9**:*650*
snowmobiles **9**:650; **10**:750
snowplows **9**:650
snowshoes **9**:*648*
snow travel **1**:37; **7**:502, *503*; **9**:**648–650**; **10**:750
soaps **2**:*146*
sodium **6**:444–445
  production **3**:225
sodium hydroxide (caustic soda) **2**:141
software and programming **3**:170; **9**:**651–653**
  and computer viruses **8**:630
soil
  archeology and **1**:51
  nitrogen **3**:185; **4**:264
soil science **9**:654
Sojourner Rover (robot) **8**:*609*
solar cells **8**:633; **9**:655, 656
solar panels **5**:*338*, 341
  on satellites **8**:623
solar power **3**:216; **4**:*245*, 246; **9**:**655–656**
  for satellites **8**:623
solar wind, solar sails using **9**:664
soldering **4**:263
solenoids **3**:227–228
solid sets **5**:386
sonar **1**:*15*
  archeology and **1**:50

for fishing **4**:279
for navigation **9**:695
sonic booms **1**:18, *19*
sound
  and Doppler effect **8**:579
  and electricity **6**:453
  frequency **8**:579
  speed **10**:783
  study of *see* acoustics
soundproofing **5**:368
sound recording **9**:**657–661**
  for movies **6**:475
South Fork Dam **3**:191
sowing **3**:184
soy foods **4**:294
space-based lasers (SBLs) **9**:693
space flight **9**:**662–664**
space frames **2**:112
space ports *see* launch sites
space probes **9**:662–663, **665–669**
space shuttles **9**:662, *670*, *674*, *676–677*
  launching **5**:393–*394*, 397; **9**:662, *676*
  propellants **4**:*303*, 305
  reentry **9**:664, *676*
  tiles **2**:*130*, 131
space stations **8**:625; **9**:**670–673**
  International Space Station **4**:*252*; **8**:625; **9**:*672*–673
space suits **9**:663, *664*, *677*–678
space travel **9**:**674–679**
  rockets for **8**:611–612, 613, *614*–615
  see also space probes; space shuttles
space walks **9**:677–*678*

Spandex **10**:738
Spangler, James Murray **10**:760
spark plugs **1**:57; **4**:249, 251; **5**:*363*
speech, recognition and synthesis **10**:*769*
speed **6**:431
speedometers **10**:753
Sperry, Elmer **6**:466; **7**:495
sphygmomanometers **3**:204; **6**:439
spin dryers **2**:128
spinnerets **4**:270
spinning **4**:268; **9**:*712*; **10**:738
spirits **1**:74–75
spoil
  from dredging **3**:209
  removal **3**:178
spoilers **8**:577
spokeshaves **10**:797–798
sports technology **9**:**680–681**
springs, hot **2**:*90*; **4**:317, *318*; **5**:341
sprinklers **5**:*384*, 386–387
Sprinter 308E (electric vehicle) **3**:*223*
Spruce Goose (flying boat) **8**:626
Sputnik satellites **9**:674–675
sputtering **5**:370
stabilizer bars **1**:63
stalling, aircraft **4**:*283*, 284–285
staples, surgical **9**:706
starch **2**:139
Stardust (space probe) **9**:669
Star Wars (film) **1**:41; **6**:478
"Star Wars" (SDI system) **9**:693
Steadicams **6**:478

stealth aircraft **1**:*26*, 28; **3**:229; **4**:287; **8**:578
steam engines **4**:248–249, *250*; **9**:**682–687**, 712
  for road vehicles **9**:686–687
  for ships and boats **6**:421–422; **8**:564; **9**:*685*, *686*, 687
  in steam locomotives **8**:587; **9**:*682*
  world's first **2**:92
  see also railroad
steel *see* iron and steel
steelyards **10**:786
steering
  automobiles **1**:59, **60–61**
  power **1**:61
  tanks **10**:749
Steiner, Rudolf **7**:518
Stephenson, George **8**:587
sterilization
  of food **4**:288
  of germs **1**:46–47; **6**:*442*
stethoscopes **6**:438
Stevens, John F. **2**:116
Stevens, Robert L. **8**:589–590
Stevenson screens **6**:451
stitches, surgical **9**:706
stock cars **8**:577
stock control **8**:599
stone, building in **2**:110
Stone Age **9**:710
stoneware **7**:557
stopcocks **10**:762
storage media **9**:**688–689**
stoves and ovens **5**:339; **9**:**690–691**
  microwave ovens **5**:*353*; **9**:*691*
strategic defense systems **9**:**692–693**
streamlining **1**:*17*, 18
streetcars **9**:694
streptomycin **1**:44
strips, bimetallic **10**:742
Stuart Little (film) **1**:*41*
styrene **2**:138

Volume numbers are in **boldface type** followed by colons. Page numbers in **boldface type** refer to main articles and their illustrations; page numbers in *italic type* refer to picture captions.

submarines 9:695–697
  depth charges and 10:747
  miniature 9:696
  nuclear 6:421, 423; 7:499;
    9:696, 697
  see also submersibles
submersibles 3:193, 195;
    9:696
  see also submarines
subsoilers 3:184
substations, electrical 3:218
subway systems 8:587;
    9:698–701
  driverless trains 8:607
Suez Canal 2:115; 3:208
sugar, processing
    4:292–293, 294
sugarcane, fuel from 4:305
sugaring, food 4:289
Suisei (space probe) 9:669
sulfides 7:516
sulfonamides 1:45
sulfur dioxide, and acid rain
    7:549; 8:567
sulfuric acid 2:140–141
Sun
  energy from 4:245
  heat from 5:341
  navigation by 7:493
  nuclear fusion 7:499
  see also solar power
sundials 10:743
superalloys 1:34
supercarriers 1:25
superconductors 2:141
supertankers 2:123; 7:515,
    551
  offshore moorings 7:513
surface coatings 7:521
surfactants 2:146, 147;
    7:521
surgery 6:441–443;
    9:702–706
  cancer 2:120–121
  cosmetic 9:706
  cryosurgery 6:442
  diagnostic 9:704
  heart-lung machines
    5:335–336

keyhole 6:437, 442–443;
    9:704
  laser 5:390–391; 9:705
surveying 9:707–709
Surveyor space probes
    9:666
suspension systems
  automobile 1:62–63
  bicycle 1:78
Swan, Joseph 9:712
switch engines 8:586
synthesizers 7:487

Tablets, medical 7:530
Tacoma Narrows Bridge
    1:18; 2:106
tags, electronic 8:628, 629
tambourines 7:489
tankers 2:123; 7:514–515,
    551
  offshore moorings 7:513
tanks 7:502; 10:748,
    749–750
  and antitank shells 2:95
tannins 5:398; 7:531
tape
  digital audio (DAT) 9:660
  magnetic 9:659–660
tape measures 9:707
tape recorders 9:688
tar sands 7:509
Tay Bridge disaster 2:106
T-cells, helper 5:365
TCP/IP 5:373
tea 1:72
  plantations 3:184
Technicolor 6:477
technology, history of
    9:710–713
Teflon 7:544
telecommunications
    9:714–718
  computer networks 3:167;
    9:717–718
  see also antennae;
    telephony and
    telegraphy; television;
    wireless
    communications

telemedicine 6:439
telephony and telegraphy
    8:583; 9:714–716;
    10:724–727
  cellular phones 1:42;
    3:167, 206–207;
    8:582; 9:716–717;
    10:726–727, 795
  Internet 5:373
  optical fibers 4:267;
    9:716; 10:726
  satellite phones 3:167;
    10:727, 795
  telegraphy for railroad
    safety 8:592
  telegraphy to "wire"
    money 1:69
  telephone exchanges
    10:725
  telephone networks
    3:166–167
  videophones 1:43; 9:717,
    718; 10:727
telescopes 10:728–730
telesurgery 6:442
television 9:717;
    10:731–736
  amplifiers 1:35
  antennae 10:732, 733
  cameras 10:734
  cathode ray tubes 3:234,
    235; 10:733, 735
  closed-circuit (CCTV)
    8:627, 628; 9:717

color 10:731–732, 733
  digital 3:207; 10:736
  electromagnets 6:420;
    10:733
  flat panel 10:736
  Internet 10:732
  plasma 10:736
  remote-control 10:753
Telford, Thomas 2:143
temperature
  and global warming
    2:154; 4:245,
    246–247, 305; 7:549;
    8:568
  measurement see
    thermometry
Tencel 4:270
Tereshkova, Valentina 9:675
terraces, farming on 3:185
terracotta army 7:556
Terylene 4:271
tetraethyl lead 4:309
textiles 10:737–740
  dyeing 3:211
  see also clothing industry;
    fibers and yarns
TGVs (trains à grande
    vitesse) 8:588

In running, a boat sails downwind; in reaching, it sails across the wind. To sail into the wind, a boat must zigzag.

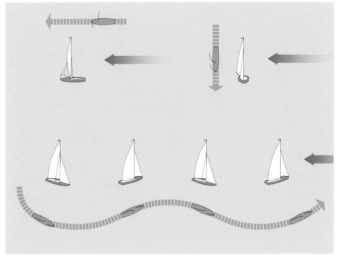

Thames Barrier **10**:762, *778*

theodolites **9**:*707, 708*

thermocouples **6**:450; **10**:742

thermography **10**:742

thermometry **6**:450; **10**:**741–742**

thermoplastics **1**:16; **7**:542, 546

thermos bottles **5**:368

thermosetting plastics (thermosets) **1**:16; **7**:542–543

threshing **5**:332

throttle **4**:251

thrust **4**:282–283, 311

tidal energy **10**:777

tie rods **1**:61

tillage **3**:184

tillers **9**:645

tills **8**:598

time **10**:**743–745**

tin **6**:447

tires **8**:617; **10**:**746**
    automobile **1**:59; **8**:617; **10**:761, 789
    pneumatic **1**:76; **10**:746
    racing **8**:577

Titanic (ship) **8**:638

titanium, in aircraft construction **1**:28

Titan rockets **5**:396

TNT (trinitrotoluene) **2**:94; **4**:258

toads, cane **2**:*85*

toasters **3**:227–228

tomatoes, genetically modified **4**:315

tomosynthesis **3**:198

Tom Thumb (locomotive) **8**:590

tools
    hand **5**:**330–331**
    invention **5**:375
    machine **6**:**416–417**
    power tools **10**:798

toothbrushes, electric **5**:353

toothpaste **1**:12, 13

Top Fuel cars **8**:577

torpedoes and depth charges **10**:**747**

torque **3**:221; **5**:342

torsion bars **1**:62, *63*

total stations **9**:708–709

Tour de France **1**:77

Townes, Charles H. **5**:390

Toy Story (film) **1**:41; **3**:177

tracked vehicles **10**:**748–750**
    for farming **10**:750, 751
    for snow **9**:*650*; **10**:750

tractors (farming) **7**:502; **10**:748, **751–752**

tractors (parts of trucks) **10**:*754–755*

trains
    diesel **8**:587–588
    driverless **8**:588, *607*
    electric **6**:427; **8**:*588*
    freight **8**:585–586, 588, *593*
    high-speed electric **6**:427; **8**:*588*
    light-rail systems **8**:587, *607*; **9**:700
    maglev **6**:*418*, 419
    railroad cars **8**:**585–588**
    steam **8**:587; **9**:*682*
    subway **8**:607; **9**:700
    see also railroad construction

tranquilizers **7**:534

Trans-Alaska pipeline **7**:515

transducers **6**:453; **10**:725, **753**

transformers **3**:217–218, 232

transfusions, blood **2**:**93**

transgenic organisms **4**:315–*316*

transistors **3**:230, 231–232, *233*; **8**:633; **10**:795
    and nanotechnology **7**:490, 491

transits **9**:708

Trans-Ko'Olau Tunnel **10**:757

transmission, mechanical *see* mechanical transmission

transmission electron microscopes (TEMs) **6**:*457*, 458

transmitters (antennae) **1**:*42–43*
    television **10**:732, *733*

transplants, organ **5**:366; **9**:704

traps, geological **7**:*505*

trawlers **4**:*279, 280, 281*

trees
    and dendrochronology **1**:*51*
    rubber **8**:*616*, 617
    see also forestry

trephination **9**:702

Trevithick, Richard **8**:587; **9**:686

triangulation **9**:707, 708, 709

triazines **7**:528

trinitrotoluene (TNT) **4**:258

triodes **3**:230, 234–235; **10**:736

tritium **7**:501

Triton (submarine) **9**:695

trombones **7**:488

trucks **10**:**754–755**
    brakes **2**:97
    construction trucks **10**:755
    dump **3**:180; **5**:*357*; **10**:755

weighing (weigh bridges) **10**:787

trusses **4**:262

Tsiolkovsky, Konstantin **8**:612; **9**:675

tug boats **7**:552

tumbling mills **1**:13

tunnels **10**:**756–757**
    canals **2**:116
    construction **5**:329; **6**:427, *428*; **9**:698–700
    GPS **5**:329
    see also civil engineering; subway systems

turbines **10**:**758–759**
    gas *see* gas turbines and engines
    reaction and impulse **10**:758
    steam **3**:236; **6**:421; **8**:567, 568; **9**:684, *687*; **10**:759
    water **5**:358, *359*; **8**:566; **10**:758–759, 776
    wind **10**:759, 790, 791, *792*

Turbinia (steam boat) **9**:687

Turbosails **6**:422

Turing, Alan **1**:53; **3**:170

Turing Test **1**:53, 54

Turtle (submarine) **9**:695

twins **2**:148

Tyndall, John **4**:266

typesetting **8**:569–571

Typhoon submarines **9**:697

tyrian purple **3**:210

U-boats **9**:695

ultracentrifuges **2**:128, 129

ultrasonic machining **6**:417

ultrasound **1**:15
    scans **3**:205; **6**:436–437, 439

ultraviolet light **3**:*164*; **6**:*411*
    for sterilization **1**:47
    telescopes **10**:730

Uniform Resource Locators (URLs) **5**:374

Volume numbers are in **boldface type** followed by colons. Page numbers in **boldface type** refer to main articles and their illustrations; page numbers in *italic type* refer to picture captions.

unpiloted aerial vehicles (UAVs) *see* drone aircraft
uranium
and atomic bombs **7**:500
isotopes **2**:129; **7**:498, 499
urine, testing **3**:204–205
URLs (Uniform Resource Locators) **5**:374

V-1 missiles **6**:468
V-2 rockets **6**:*468*; **8**:613, *614*, 615
vaccination **5**:*364*, 365, *366*; **10**:764
vacuum cleaners **5**:353; **10**:760
vacuum tubes **3**:234, 235
in computers **3**:174
Vaiont Dam **3**:191
Valium **7**:534
valves **10**:761–762
butterfly **10**:761
diaphragm **10**:761–762
float **10**:762
gate **10**:*762*
globe **10**:761
needle **10**:762
poppet (mushroom valves) **10**:761
slide **10**:762
stopcocks **10**:762
varnishes **7**:521
vaults (arches) **2**:109
veal **6**:412
Vega space probes **9**:667
vegetables
harvesting **5**:333
processing **4**:288–289
see also horticulture
veneer **10**:797
Venera space probes **9**:666–667
ventilating machines **5**:*371*
ventilation systems (air conditioning) **1**:19
subway **9**:*699*, 701
Venus, space probes to **9**:*666*–667

veterinary medicine **10**:763–765
see also livestock farming
videography **10**:766–768
holovideo **5**:347
streaming video **10**:732, 767
surveillance systems **8**:628
video cassette recorders (VCRs) **9**:688; **10**:*766*–767
videophones **1**:43; **9**:717, *718*; **10**:727
Vietnam War, hovercraft **5**:354
Viking space probes **9**:667
virtual reality markup language (VRML) **7**:485
viruses, computer **8**:630
viscose process **4**:270
vision **3**:164
vitamins **4**:293
viticulture **1**:73
vitrification **7**:557
voice recognition **10**:769
Volta, Alessandro **3**:224–225
voltage **3**:214
voltaic piles **3**:225
von Braun, Wernher **8**:613, 615
vortex generators **4**:284–285
Voyager space probes **9**:*663*, 666
VRML (virtual reality markup language) **7**:485
VS-100 (helicopter) **5**:343, *344*
V/STOL aircraft **1**:25
vulcanization **8**:617; **10**:746

Walls
cavity **2**:*101*
dry-stone **2**:110
WANs (wide area networks) **3**:167

washing machines **5**:352
washing machines and dishwashers **10**:770–771
wasps, parasitic **2**:84–85; **3**:187
waste treatment **10**:772–775
hazardous waste **5**:334
landfills **5**:334; **7**:549; **10**:772
watches **10**:743–*744*, 745
water hyacinths **2**:84
water jets, for marine propulsion **6**:422
water power **10**:776–777
see also hydroelectricity
water resources **10**:778–781
waterwheels **10**:776, 777
Watson-Watt, Robert **8**:578
Watt, James **9**:686, 687
watts **3**:218
wavelength **3**:164; **5**:389; **6**:404; **10**:783
wave motion **10**:782–783
wave power **10**:784–785
weather
balloons **1**:67
chaos theory and **2**:*132*
forecasting **6**:451; **8**:*622*
weaving **10**:738–739
weigh bridges **10**:787

weightlessness, in space **9**:*662*, 664
weights and measures **10**:786–787
see also measurement
welding **4**:263
wells **10**:*780*
welting **4**:295
Westinghouse, George **8**:585; **9**:687
whaling **4**:280
wheat **1**:64
Wheatstone, Charles **10**:724
wheels **1**:37; **6**:433; **9**:710; **10**:788–789
see also tires
whiskey **1**:74–75
Whitehead, Robert **10**:747
Whitney, Eli **9**:713
Whittle, Frank **6**:*427*, 428
wide area networks (WANs) **3**:167; **5**:372
windmills **10**:758, *790*, 791–792
see also wind power
wind power **3**:216; **4**:247; **10**:759, **790–792**

The blades of a turbine turn to create energy, which is harnessed to drive whatever the turbine is powering.

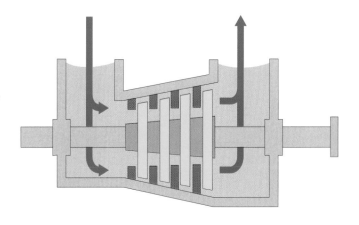

wind speed, measuring **6**:450–*451*
wind tunnels **1**:*18*, 19; **4**:253
wine **1**:*73–74*
winnowing **5**:332
wireless communication **10:793–795**
see also antennae; radio; television
wirephotos **4**:260
Wise, John **1**:66
woad **3**:211
wood and wood carving **5**:331; **10:796–798**
building with wood **2**:108–109
cellulose from wood **4**:270
dating, archeology (dendrochronology) **1**:*51*
paper from wood pulp **7**:524
wood as a fuel **4**:246, 305

see also forestry
wool **4**:268, 269, 271; **10**:738
dyeing **3**:211
see also clothing; textiles
Woolf, Arthur **9**:687
Woolworth Building **9**:646
word processors **9**:653
see also computers
workstations **3**:177
World War I
tracked vehicles **10**:748, 750
zeppelins **1**:67
World War II
amphibious trucks **7**:*502*
attack on Pearl Harbor **1**:24

Liberty ships **8**:635
nuclear weapons **7**:500
radio **8**:583
submarines **9**:695
World Wide Web (WWW) **3**:175; **5**:372, 374; **7**:485
wrecking balls **3**:197
Wright, Frank Lloyd **2**:111
Wright, Orville and Wilbur **1**:30; **4**:286; **6**:427; **9**:713
WWW see World Wide Web

Xenon **4**:308
xerography **7**:535
X rays **3**:198, 205; **6**:*434*, *437*, 439, *443*
for sterilization **1**:47
telescopes **10**:730
see also computed tomography
xylophones **7**:489

Yachts **8**:619
Yale, Linus, Jr. **6**:414, 415
yards (unit of measurement) **6**:425
yarns see fibers and yarns
yaw **4**:*282*, 285
yeast, and baking **1**:64–65
Young, Arthur **5**:344

Zeiss, Carl **5**:326
zeolites **2**:125
zeppelins **1**:*67*
zinc **6**:447
zip disks **3**:173; **9**:689
zoetropes **6**:473
zoonoses **10**:765
Zuider Zee **2**:143

Volume numbers are in **boldface type** followed by colons. Page numbers in **boldface type** refer to main articles and their illustrations; page numbers in *italic type* refer to picture captions.

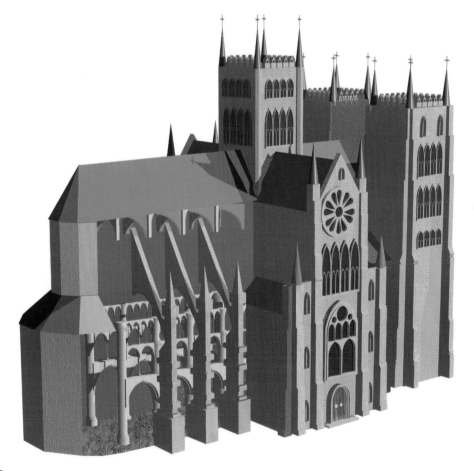

The medieval Gothic cathedrals of Europe, such as this one, are among the most spectacular stone buildings ever constructed. It was difficult to design buildings with massive walls and roofs that could support their own weight. Architects solved this problem by building arches and massive supports called flying buttresses.